THE HUNGARIAN NATIONAL MUSEUM

THE HUNGARIAN NATIONAL MUSEUM

Published for the 175th Anniversary
of the Museum

CORVINA PRESS

Title of the original: A Magyar Nemzeti Múzeum —
Megjelent a Múzeum alapításának 175. évfordulójára
Corvina Kiadó, Budapest 1977

Edited by
FERENC FÜLEP

Translated by Elisabeth Hoch
Colour photographs by Károly Szelényi
Black-and-white photographs by Kálmán Kónya
Photographs No. 154 by Lajos Dobos, No. 143 by József Karáth and
Nos. 142, 145 by Alfréd Schiller
Binding and jacket by János Szilassy

Printed in Hungary, 1978
Kossuth Printing House, Budapest

INTRODUCTION

The Hungarian National Museum, one of the outstanding institutions of Hungarian cultural and scientific life is 175 years old. It was founded in the first half of the nineteenth century as part of a movement to preserve Hungarian historic traditions and to instill greater appreciation of the Hungarian language and culture. This movement was influenced by the ideals of the Enlightenment, and the National Museum was one of its first fruits. Today it ranks among the oldest museums in the world.

Since the foundation of the museum, its fate has been linked with the history of Hungary. During 1848–1849 it was the vanguard of the progressive elements. In the second half of the century, well-known scientists, men of national and international authority, prominent scholars and organizers of scientific life, guided its development. After Hungary's millenary celebrations in 1896 the National Museum celebrated its own centenary. Later, at the time of the Hungarian Republic of Councils, in 1919 the museum staff and workers endeavoured to open its doors to the people at large. Under the Horthy regime, it shared in the general decline of scientific and cultural institutions. After the Liberation of Hungary in 1945, though severely damaged, the National Museum led the reorganization of museology in Hungary. Once again progressive science thrived within its walls; its didactic exhibitions established a new school of thought both at home and abroad and, visited by masses of people, it soon became the home of public education. Today it still plays a significant role in the development of historic consciousness of the Hungarian people and in the preservation of national traditions.

The Hungarian National Museum once housed the collections of several large Budapest museums. Today these independent museums, having branched off from the founding institution, preserve important special collections. Until 1949 the Széchényi Library also belonged to the museum. The material of the National Museum includes archaeological and historical remains found in Hungary and dating from the Palaeolithic Age through the Middle Ages. Some departments contain items which pertain to Hungary's history in chronological order. Traces of old traditions remain in the organization of the museum, for some departments follow a chronological order, while certain special collections present a historical cross-section. To keep pace with newer developments in museology, the museum has recently established a Public Education Department which will forge contacts with schools, centres of mass communication, and the general public.

The fifty-member scientific research team of the National Museum forms the nucleus of the archaeological, numismatic and historic research work carried on in Hungary. Its members are the heads of important archaeological excavations, the authors of numerous Hungarian books and publications and the participants of a wide range of Hungarian and international conventions. The international reputation and prestige of the National Museum is confirmed by its contact with nearly 600 foreign institutions, and by its highly qualified research workers, who hold various Hungarian and foreign degrees, and who are members of scientific societies and institutions as well.

In the past 175 years, the small sapling that was planted in 1802 has grown into a huge tree with wide-spreading branches. It gives today's scholars as well as the entire staff of the museum great pleasure and pride to see the progress that has been made during the thirty years since the Liberation of the country. There has been growth both in the museum's collections and in the number of its research workers, improvement in the research conditions, better financed facilities and an increase in the number of visitors. All this has occurred for one reason; since the Liberation in 1945 the people of Hungary consider the National Museum as their own, and they appreciate it as an important organization devoted to preserving their national heritage. These sentiments constitute a pledge for the further development of the National Museum as it approaches its bicentenary.

Ferenc Fülep

THE HISTORY OF THE HUNGARIAN
NATIONAL MUSEUM

Because of Hungary's historical situation as a part of the Habsburg Empire, no royal collection which could have formed the basis of a national public collection was able to exist after the middle of the eighteenth century. At this period industry was still functioning within the framework of the guilds and the middle classes had not yet begun to play an important role in society. The majority of the members of the aristocracy were seeking favours at the Viennese court; the country gentry were becoming more and more impoverished and works of art flowed continuously from every country within the Empire into the imperial collection in Vienna.

Both the spread of the Enlightenment and the influence of the French Revolution had aroused in Hungary aspirations directed at the formation of a national state, as they had elsewhere. Hungary's foremost ambitions were directed towards the establishment of an indigenous system of education, the use of the Hungarian language in official circles and the worthy presentation of the nation's historic treasures. The university, until that time the highest institute of learning, no longer appeared sufficient to meet these aims. To promote research and proper standards of education, the bourgeois society established academies, libraries and museums. Attempts towards the development of an independent state are always accompanied by moves towards the establishment of a national museum which will embody both its history and its character, as well as constituting a concomitant of its pursuit of national unity in its struggles towards independence. The spokesmen who urged the use of the national language and the preservation of the nation's culture were the gentry but, in view of their financial situation, the founders of the collections themselves were, naturally, the aristocracy. An outstanding figure among these last was the West-Transdanubian nobleman, Count Ferenc Széchényi (1754–1820), who deliberately built up a collection in order to further his country's education, a collection which was to form the foundation of the nation's museum. In his public career, Count Széchényi was soon confronted with the social inconsistencies of his period, with the result that he withdrew from public life to devote himself to the formation of a collection, for which purpose he employed as his librarian József Hajnóczy, later a leader of the Hungarian Jacobin movement. He was also helped in building up his collection by István Schönwisner, a pioneer in the field of archaeology and numismatics, by Károly Alma in heraldry and by Márton György Kovachich in diplomacy. On November 25, 1802, he considered the time to be ripe for presenting to his country the Hungarian material he had collected with such great pains and with such considerable sacrifice since his early youth. It consisted of 11,884 printed documents, 1,150 manuscripts, 142 volumes of maps and copper engravings, 2,209 coats of arms, 2,655 medals, 702 of which were gold, various antiques and a number of portraits. Széchényi's collection was not by any means the richest in Hungary, it was far surpassed in value by the Viczai Collection preserved at Hédervár, Sámuel Teleki's library at Marosvásárhely (Tîrgu Mureş) and the private collections of several members of the Hungarian aristocracy, among them the Esterházys, living in Vienna.

Széchényi's efforts to continue to enrich the collections so far as his means would allow even after he had donated them to the nation, and the fact that he published catalogues of them at his own expense, raise him far above his contemporaries. Literary and scientific circles in Hungary, as well as over the whole of Central Europe, received the news of his foundation with the greatest enthusiasm, all the more so since it was the first of its kind in this area. The nation assumed possession of the new institution at the following National Assembly in 1807, immortalizing Ferenc Széchényi's name and paying tribute to his merit.

According to the deed of the foundation, control of the collection was entrusted to the Palatine Joseph, a progressive member of the Habsburg family, a choice which ensured a part of the costs of maintenance as being covered by state subsidy. The Palatine Joseph met his responsibilities in a manner worthy of his dignity; he performed his duties as supervisor of the institution for nearly fifty years.

The museum was opened in the Pest Paulite monastery on December 10, 1803. It consisted of a library, a reading room and rooms for the exhibition of medals and antiquities. Among the many vital problems which faced the new institution the most pressing was the necessity to stop the privileges ensured to Viennese collectors; to develop Hungarian collections and to build a new home for the museum.

According to the dispositions of the Viennese Chancellery, surviving from the eighteenth century, the Hungarian state was to have a one-third share of the treasures found on her territory while all archaeological and numismatic finds were to be sent first to Vienna for selection. This state of affairs ceased

Portrait of Ferenc Széchényi. After a painting by Sámuel Czetter

only in 1867, when it was allowed that finds need no longer be sent to Vienna but could be redeemed by the Hungarian National Museum.

In order to raise funds for the further development of the existing collections, the Palatine Joseph tried to enlist the co-operation of the nobility. The first director of the museum, Ferdinand Miller, drew up in detail the programme in the Latin Museum Hungaricum and in the Hungarian Nemzeti Gyűjtemények (National Collections) designed for presentation to the National Assembly of 1807, when the author attempted to prevail upon the wealthy to support the venture by appealing to their sense of national honour. He composed an outline of what the national repository was to contain and, in accordance with the ideas of the age, suggested the especial development of the following collections: (1) Medals; (2) Antiquities and rarities; (3) Weapons; (4) Marble and stone objects; (5) Crafts, in particular collections designed to further industrial and commercial education; (6) Picture gallery, containing portraits of Hungary's historical ancestors; (7) Natural resources.

Széchényi's example found few followers. Most of the two hundred and thirty-one donors who came forward before 1821 came from the ranks of the bourgeoisie—the civil servants—a social class which felt most strongly that the museum was its own. Nevertheless, the museum's circle of collectors steadily widened, even though the pace was slow. In 1808 Ferenc Széchényi's wife, Júlia Festetich, presented her rich collection of minerals, thereby establishing the Collection of Natural Resources, the ancestor of today's Natural History Museum. The Collection of Medals and Antiquities, the direct ancestor of today's National Museum, was promoted to the status of a museum department in 1814.

The museum's second home was the former central building of the University which was opened to the public on June 30, 1811. During all this time, however, the Palatine Joseph never ceased to plead for the construction of a museum building designed specifically to house the growing collections.

The National Assembly of 1832–1836 achieved two notable results. In the first place it approved the purchase of the Miklós Jankovich Collection which included 63,000 books, 1,266 specimens of goldsmiths' work, 174 weapons and 7,000 medals, all of which formed the basis of the collection devoted to Hungary's cultural history; but in the second place, the Assembly also passed a bill allocating 500,000 forints for the purpose of erecting a building which was to be the new museum. Its design was entrusted to the Pest architect Mihály Pollack (1773–1854). Both the employers and the architect were well aware that their task was to raise a monument destined to endure for centuries

10

Portrait of Mihály Pollack. Oil painting by Mór Than (around 1880)

and that they were looked to to create an embodiment of the nation's aspirations in the field of cultural development.

The present building, erected between 1837 and 1847, with this object in mind, was indeed monumental as compared with the size of Pest at that time. Designed in the Neo-Classical style, the eight-column portico of the building, covering 109×70 metres, is surmounted by a tympanum decorated with the allegorical figures of Science, Art, History and Fame. The harmoniously conceived exterior leads into the spacious interior, which was, however, more modest when it was completed than had been originally intended. Lack of funds dictated its final form and, in fact, the interior decoration was not completed until the 1870s, with the painting of the frescoes by Károly Lotz and Mór Than.

The planning of the museum's equipment had to be shouldered by the museum's second director, Ágoston Kubinyi (1799–1873). He was the first to emphasize the importance of public education as a major part of the museum's programme. In 1846 he introduced what was then a modern catalogue in Hungarian. To further enrich the archaeological collection he took the initiative of launching new excavations, the first of which was the excavation of the royal tombs at Székesfehérvár, under the direction of Érdy-Lutzenbacher in 1848.

The museum building played an important part, at the end of the Reform Era, in the events of the 1848 bourgeois Revolution. It was on the steps of the museum that Sándor Petőfi's *National Song* was first recited; the Upper House of the National Assembly met in the museum's state apartment; exhibitions on industrial and agricultural production, designed to rouse the whole country, were held in its galleries. The most important of the gatherings of unions and associations, formed for the promotion of public education, were also held within its walls, all of which tended to establish the museum as the centre of Hungary's cultural and scientific life.

The defeat of the War of Independence of 1848–49 was followed by difficult times. Material means for the running of the museum were lacking and, at the same time, the institution was burdened with heavy taxes. Collective action, however, came to its aid. Saplings to plant in the grounds surrounding the museum were collected from sixty-three counties and the proceeds of concerts conducted by Ferenc Liszt and Ferenc Erkel were allocated for the purpose of designing a park for the museum, which was then situated on the fringe of the city.

The rapid development of capitalism which followed the agreement ar-

The Hungarian National Museum
Festive procession of Kossuth's canvassers before the Hungarian National Museum
(F. Weiss)

ranged between nation and ruler in 1867 opened a new era for the museum. It was required to undertake a twofold task, which took the form, in the first place, of the cultivation of its scientific aspects by specialists. This work was raised to European standards by the activities of the trio of archaeologists and art historians, Ferenc Pulszky (1814–1897), Flóris Rómer (1815–1889) and József Hampel (1849–1913). In recognition of their work, the museum made its premises available for the 8th International Anthropological and Archaeological Congress of 1876, which established the international reputation of Hungarian archaeology.

In 1870 the museum had eight departments: Medals, Antiquities, Pictures, Ethnography, Zoology and Botany, Palaeontology, Handicrafts and the Széchényi Library.

The development of individual sciences broke through the museum's earlier framework and, with the secession of the departments of handicrafts, the process began of branching-off single departments from the mother-institute. In 1873, on the initiative of the National Industrial Association, the National Hungarian Museum of Arts and Crafts came into being. The Ethnographic Department, which became an independent unit in 1872, was enriched by the addition of the foreign collections of Antal Reguly and János Xántus. In 1871 the Hungarian State purchased the Esterházy Collection which formed the foundation of the National Gallery and later of the Museum of Fine Arts. The Historical Gallery was established as a part of the preparations for the millennial festivities, which were then imminent. In 1934, after many vicissitudes, this institution was at last integrated into the organization of the Hungarian National Museum.

Following the separation of the collections of fine art, crafts and ethnography, the museum's activities centred round research in the fields of archaeology, numismatics and cultural history. Due to lack of a nation-wide interest the flow of new acquisitions slowed down considerably, and because the museum appeared to cater only to the interests of connoisseurs, it became isolated from the life of the city.

In the eyes of the progressive middle classes the Hungarian National Museum glorified the nation's past and the people's love of the country; for the ruling class it was a remote national shrine. It had been in the vestibule of the museum that Lajos Kossuth had lain in state in 1894; here the mortal remains of Ferenc Rákóczi II rested on their way to Kassa (Košice) in 1906, and from here the poet, Endre Ady, was accompanied in 1919 by hundreds of thousands of people on his last journey.

Main staircase of the Hungarian National Museum

The fact that at this period the museum tended to satisfy only the interests of a limited circle and failed to find a place in the education of society as a whole meant that its activities sank to their lowest level, both as regards their form and their effect on the community. It was the cultural policy of the Hungarian Republic of Councils, proclaimed in the spring of 1919, which was to afford an escape from this situation by setting the museum three major tasks:

1) The introduction, in the museum's scientific work, of Marxist scientific principles and the accumulating of collections to effect this end.

2) The ending of a situation by which the museums served only their own advancement and the turning of all these institutions into places of public education.

3) To increase an awareness and appreciation of the nation's treasures and the termination of all privileges attached to private ownership.

The reorganization of the Hungarian National Museum, which had its own historic past, proved to be the most difficult problem set before it. After several plans had been considered it was agreed that a Museum of Cultural History should take its place. The Hungarian Republic of Councils's 133 days' rule, proved, however, insufficient to overcome inner resistance which was maintained against these measures. A more promising plan appeared to be to seek out new forms of public education, in which the principal endeavour should be to use the study of the cultures of the past as a means of introducing socialist principles. Furthermore the museum should undertake the important task of raising educational standards as applied to the whole community. By extending the opening hours of the museum and by organizing courses for working people, by establishing academies, museum lectures and excursions, every attempt was made to open up new vistas to replace the closed world which had been characteristic of the museum before these plans came into being. The nationalization of private collections also proved fruitful, although the very limited principles on which most of these had been based meant that they did not make an appreciable contribution to the museum's collection.

The cultural-political ideas thus formulated could not, however, be realized. The counter-revolutionary Horthy regime which came into power regarded it as one of its main tasks—apart from that of indulging in revenge—to turn the museums into organizations suitable for their own ideological purposes. Between the two World Wars they enacted three laws applying to museums; the 1922 and 1934 Acts referred to the reorganization of the Hungarian National Museum, centred round the idea of giving it autonomy, though this was, in fact, only an illusion. It was stipulated that the pursuit of the sciences

16

Detail of the Historical Exhibition at the Hungarian National Museum (1967)

should be the major undertaking of the museum and that all collections relevant to scientific aspects should be given the collective title of "The Universal Collection", concentrated under the autonomous Council of the Hungarian National Museum. Within this organization our museum was renamed the Hungarian Historical Museum, and in addition to its traditional departments—Archaeology, History, Medals and Picture Gallery—it included also the material of the Museum of Arts and Crafts and the Ethnographical Museum, both of which institutions were deprived of their independence. Additions to the collections and the organization of exhibitions were also governed by the regime's attitude to the history of ideas. The tangible relics of Hungarian history were confined to the glittering objects of the ruling classes; exhibitions relating to the history of the middle classes and the serfs were omitted.

This government failed to give the museum sufficient financial support even to enable the authorized scientific programmes to be carried out. In 1932 the Historical Museum could not afford to allocate more than the ridiculous annual sum of 87 pengős to excavations; the rest had to be raised through friendly contacts with private sources. Thanks, however, to the unremitting zeal of talented employees, scientific specialization prospered in spite of these circumstances and a series of monographs (*Archaeologia Hungarica, Bibliotheca Humanitatis Historica*) and a documentary review of current finds (*Folia Archaeologica*) were published. Before long the scientific aspects of the museum's work rose to European standards, while, at the same time, the museum's successful policy of collecting contributed to the widening of its collections, especially in the fields of archaeology and numismatics. The growing body of material soon began to present problems of storage to which extension of the building, according to designs by Jenő Lechner, proved only a temporary solution.

This era of bourgeois development closed with the heavy losses incurred by World War II. Mihály Pollack's lofty building revealed seventy-five gaping wounds inflicted by the shelling. Its walls stood stark and roofless and the dreadful siege of 1945 reduced its park to a cemetery. The day of liberation dawned on burnt-out repositories and damaged objects of art. Most regrettably in spite of careful packing and storage, ten per cent of the archaeological material was completely lost. The greatest damage was suffered by the cultural-historic material, when the largest repository was burned to the ground and the goldsmiths' work, wrought iron and textile materials as well as the musical instruments preserved in it were reduced to ashes and molten metal.

18

Detail of the Historical Exhibition at the Hungarian National Museum (1967)

At the cost of a heroic effort the museum was once more roofed in by the end of 1945, after which its workers concentrated all their endeavours towards getting the exhibition halls restored. In May 1946 the first two exhibitions opened under the titles "Soviet–Hungarian Relations" and "The American Way of Life in Pictures".

The introduction of the new currency, the forint, hastened the work of reconstruction. Further exhibition halls were restored and the repositories were equipped with the most essential furniture.

The fruits of the economic changes introduced after the country's Liberation were soon extended also into the field of culture. The year 1948 saw preparations for the reorganization of the museum's exhibition area and, with the exhibition staged to celebrate the centenary of the 1848 War of Independence, the doors of the museum were thrown open to the general public. It was a new public composed of workers and peasants who for the first time could regard the museum as an institution which was truly their own. It was at this exhibition that they could see the true story of the 1848–1849 War of Independence for the first time. The exhibition was visited by a million people in a single year.

The law applied to museums enacted in 1949 opened up new avenues for the development of the museum. It declared that all excavated source material and archaeological objects are to be regarded as the property of the state; it also introduced the concept of protected archaeological areas. Collections still in private hands were, furthermore, placed under a form of protection which enabled the authorities to use the objects in such collections for public educational purposes. The autonomy of the Hungarian National Museum was cancelled and all museums were subjected to the direction of the newly established National Centre for Museums and Monuments. The new task set for the museums was the responsibility for organizing wide-spread education, available to the public and based on their scientific researches. With this end in view the National Museum had to be reorganized and the changes took place in the year that marked the 150th anniversary of the foundation of the museum. By dividing the Historical Department into two parts, they established a Medieval History Department and a Modern History Department, the former to deal with Hungarian prehistory, the exploration of the Hungarian Conquest and the medieval villages, the latter through the collection, preservation and research into material relating to the period from the defeat of the War of Independence under the leadership of Rákóczi at the beginning of the eighteenth century up to our own days.

Visitors in front of the Hungarian National Museum (1975)

The Department of Records and Documentation was established round about the same time. In addition to the responsibility for building up the collection which related to the history of the museum, it was charged with the recording of the archaeological and numismatic material at a national level, the co-ordination of the salvaging of finds revealed in the course of preparations for building and other earthworks, and the central documentation of archaeological field-work. The foundation of the Central Archaeological Library and the fusion of the separate restoration workshops into a self-contained department also date from this time.

The results of changes in the organization, strongly directed management and increased material resources soon manifested themselves both in collecting and building up the activities of the museum, as well as in schemes of public education based on this work. As a national institute controlling the largest archaeological work-force, the National Museum was given a decisive role to play in archaeological research. It became the repository of the archaeological projects of the Hungarian Academy of Sciences and even after the establishment of the Academy's own Archaeological Institute it still remained the overall archaeological centre.

The museum's plans are directed towards a large variety of targets including the archaeological exploration and rescue excavations in the areas of important building operations. The museum is also one of the centres which issues publications dealing with archaeology. The *Archaeologiai Értesítő*, first published in 1868, is still, today, edited in the museum although from the point of view of its organization it is the responsibility of the Academy within whose terms of reference it falls. The *Numizmatikai Közlöny* published by the Numismatic Society since 1902 is also edited in the museum, which is the venue of practically all the important publications on the subject in Hungary. Further, *Folia Archaeologica* is published by the museum and, since 1972, also the *Folia Historica*, which covers research into historical matters. The *Régészeti Füzetek* series No. I contains articles on archaeological field-work, while series No. II covers information on documentary sources. As a result of the research conducted by members of the museum staff the size of its collections has doubled in the course of the past thirty years. All these circumstances have enabled the museum to mount exhibitions based on its new outlook and the new methods it is employing. Since the Liberation of Hungary in 1945, the history of the peoples inhabiting her territories has been presented in three permanent archaeological exhibitions—those of 1950, 1961 and 1977. Rather than catering exclusively for specialists, the museum's archaeologists took, in these exhibitions, the first steps towards the staging of exhibitions suitable for the education of the majority of the people; in this they have established a high reputation for Hungarian exhibitions based on didactic methods. The absence from the collections of material relevant to the lives of the ordinary people has been compensated for by the museum's medieval finds.

A leading role has also been played by the Museum in research into Hungary's prehistory and the history of the Hungarian Conquest and, furthermore, in the exploration of the sites of medieval villages and in the solution of other problems connected with the country's history.

As to the modern historical collections, the earlier aim had been to increase first of all the collections of textiles and weapons, but as support for historical material increased so did collections in other areas with the result that the complex collections relevant to the past hundred years is significant. As the results of research carried out in the fields of history and economic and social history grew in importance, the National Museum's standing among similar institutions elsewhere in the world increased. The permanent exhibitions of historical material (1952 and 1967), based on the collections and their analysis, present the history of Hungary from the Conquest of the Carpathian Basin to 1849. From among the representative exhibitions mounted to mark occasions of important historic anniversaries, outstanding public success was achieved by those commemorating the 250th anniversary (1953) of the War of Independence led by Rákóczi, the 500th anniversary (1956) of the Nándorfehérvár (Belgrade) victory against the Turkish invasion in Europe and the 500th (1973) anniversary of the birth of György Dózsa, the leader of the peasant rebellion against the feudal system in 1514. The roughly six million people who have visited the museum since the Liberation of Hungary have been able to see more than 150 exhibitions.

Since 1963 the exhibition sites of the Vértesszőlős prehistoric man, the King Matthias Museum at Visegrád, the Rákóczi Museum at Sárospatak, the Kossuth Lajos Memorial Museum at Monok and the Károlyi Mihály Memorial Room in Budapest are also under the Museum's direction.

The Public Education Section was recently formed to satisfy the public's great interest about work in progress. Lectures given to visitors both in Hungarian and in other languages and the many well organized programmes with groups of schoolchildren and adults are all designed to increase the activities of the Hungarian National Museum.

József Korek

THE DEPARTMENTS
OF THE HUNGARIAN NATIONAL MUSEUM

Date of foundation:	Originally the Department was formed as a part of the Collection of Medals and Antiquities. Since 1926 it has functioned as a separate department.
Collections:	The Prehistoric Collection Roman Period Collection Migration Period Collection Historical Zoological Collection
Number of items:	400,280

DEPARTMENT OF ARCHAEOLOGY

The first archaeological remains which now form a part of the collection in the Department of Medals and Antiquities, founded in 1814, came from the private collection of the Museum's founder, Count Ferenc Széchényi.

Research in the field was greatly encouraged by the excavation begun in the middle of the last century and, later, the Congrès International d'Anthropologie et d'Archéologie, held in Budapest in 1876, provided archaeologists with a further powerful incentive. The contributions made by Flóris Rómer, Ferenc Pulszky and József Hampel in the service of Hungarian archaeology have given their names a permanent place in its history.

Between the two World Wars the most important work in the field of Hungarian archaeological research is linked with the names of Lajos Márton, Jenő Hillebrand, Ferenc Tompa, István Paulovics, and Nándor Fettich.

Since the end of World War II work on excavation has rapidly progressed and finds have been increasingly important and interesting. The growing complexity of research has called for the establishment of a collection of historical zoology, and palaeolithic researches have been carried out on a far more intensive scale than ever before. The most important result in this field was the finding of the remains of *Homo erectus* at the ancient site of Vértesszőlős between 1963 and 1968. The results of Hungarian research are now appearing as published reports, both in book form and as specialized and general articles in journals.

The permanent archaeological exhibition entitled "The Prehistory of the Peoples of Hungary", staged by the Archaeological Department of the Museum, was opened in 1950. New finds and progress in the work of research made a further exhibition possible in 1961, with the title "The History of the Peoples of Hungary up to the Time of the Magyar Conquest". More recent material still was made accessible to the public in 1976 and is now on show and, in addition, numerous exhibitions have been organized by the Department in Leningrad, Moscow, Munich, Prague, Stockholm and Vienna among other places.

Ilona Kovrig

1 LAUREL-LEAF SHAPED POINT

Site: Szeleta Cave, Borsod-Abaúj-Zemplén County
Inv. No.: Pb/82. Quartz porphyry
Length: 10.8 cm
Palaeolithic Age, Szeleta Culture

The exploration of the Szeleta Cave between 1906 and 1911 was the first palaeolithic excavation carried out in Hungary. In both outlook and method it determined all the undertakings of a similar nature which followed. The geologist, Ottokár Kadić, collected from the five cultural layers of the cave 1,603 tools as well as splitters and rich hordes of animal bones belonging to the early and developed Szeleta cultures.

The material culture of the bear-hunting ethnic group inhabiting the caves of the Bükk Mountains at the beginning of the last ice-age, forty thousand years ago, had its roots in the middle period of the Palaeolithic Age but later types also occur among their tools. These hunters produced their most important weapon, the spearhead, from a vitreous quartz porphyry of excellent quality. The symmetrical spearheads, carefully cut and displaying perfect workmanship are unique among the contemporary weapons in Central Europe.

2 SHELL BRACELETS

Site: Kisköre, Heves County
Inv. No.: 66.5.16; 67.9.10–11. Spondylus shell
Diameter: 7–9 cm
Neolithic Age, 26th century BC

The bracelets were found in 1963–1966, during the excavations by József Korek, in graves belonging to the Tisza Culture. Jewellery made from spondylus shells, which flourished in the temperate waters of seas such as the Aegean, were greatly in demand in the Neolithic Age. Bracelets, amulets and beads cut from these shells were transported and changed in Middle and South-East Europe from the Aegean to the territories of present-day Germany. The spondylus finds indicate a connection between the neolithic cultures of Hungary and the Aegean peoples of the same age. This connection is also testified by the similarities of the idols and other objects of the cult.

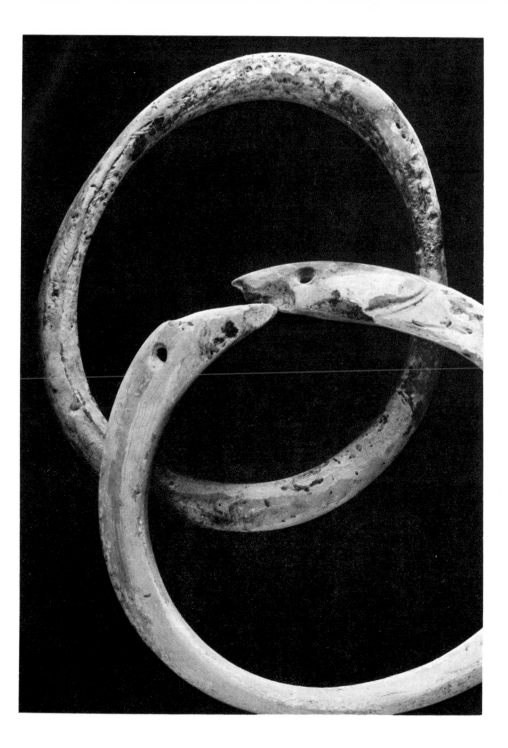

3 BOWL WITH PEDESTAL

Site: Lebő, Alsóhalom, Csongrád County
Inv. No.: 51.7.205. Pottery, yellowish-red
Height: 21.5 cm
Neolithic Age, 26th century BC

During the last phase of the Neolithic Age, Eastern Hungary was inhabited by the people of the Tisza Culture. This straight-sided bowl with a slightly outward-bending rim and an almost cylindrical pedestal was found during the excavation by József Korek in 1950 in one of the refuse pits at Lebő. It is a relict characteristic of the pottery crafts-manship of the Tisza people. Both the whole surface of the bowl itself and the pedestal are decorated with a carefully engraved meandering pattern which is completed by ornamental rows of impressed dots.

The skilfully ornamented vessels of the Tisza Culture were produced during the brightest period of neolithic economy when the inhabitants of the farming villages settled down for comparatively long periods and lived in safety in the same place. It was in these circumstances that they were able to develop a high standard of craftsmanship using ceramic, bone and stone.

4 WAGON-SHAPED VESSEL

Site: Szigetszentmárton, Pest County
Inv. No.: 72.191. Pottery, grey
Height: 9 cm
Copper Age, 22nd to 21st century BC

This funerary object belonging to the Baden Culture of the late Copper Age has come to light from a grave discovered by builders in the central area of the village of Sziget-szentmárton in 1972.

The wagon has solid wheels. The two axles extending between the wheels are joined in the middle by a rib-like tree. The strongly protruding edges of the vessel probably imitate the stay-rods supporting the sides of the carriage. The zigzag lines beside them indicate the method of fixing the corners, and the same ornament used under the curved rim suggests the suspension of the side-walls. The creator of this vessel had made an abstract representation of the elements of a wickerwork wagon-body fixed by means of flexible rods. He had not included in his model the carriage-pole but its absence is not disturbing since the handle of the vessel, starting from the rim, joins the surface above the place of the pole.

This small vessel is in many respects related to contemporary Balkan and Anatolian vessels. Together with the wagon-shaped vessel of the same period found at Budakalász, they provide the earliest proofs of the appearance of the wheeled vehicle in Europe and are thus among the most precious remains of the history of the technology. It may be presumed that the cattle-drawn wagon was introduced into the Carpathian Basin from Anatolia, carried through the Balkans by the people of the Baden Culture.

These wagon-shaped vessels may have been used for the performance of cultic ceremonies and their dispositions in graves must have had a symbolic meaning; wagons used, in fact, to facilitate the journey of the dead to the other world.

5 HUMAN-SHAPED URNS

Site: Ózd, Center, Borsod-Abaúj-Zemplén County
Inv. No.: 59.14.7–9. Pottery, dark grey
Height: 40.6, 23.9 to 48.4 cm
Copper Age, 20th century BC

The urns were found by Nándor Kalicz at Center in 1958 in one of the graves of the Late Copper Age Baden Culture. The largest among them held the ashes of an adult woman, each of the two smaller, those of a child. The grave was surrounded by stones.

The lower part of the urns forms a rounded belly; a cross-section of the upper part is a flattened oval. The mouth of both the largest and the smallest urns is closed by a protruding "roof" suggesting an ornamental head-dress of hair arrangement. The oval opening for the reception of the ashes is at the back of this piece. The third urn has a rim as is usual with such vessels.

Using a three-dimensional technique to represent eyes and breasts the potter has contrived to give these vessels, in spite of their extreme simplicity, an effectively expressive appearance.

Urns of this kind represented the dead whose ashes they contained. Similar vessels, comparable in significance to sepulchral statues, have been found in the early strata of Troy and, as the other available data, they suggest the Anatolian-Balkan origin of the Baden Culture.

6 BELL-SHAPED BEAKER

Site: Tököl, Pest County
Inv. No.: 143/1878.1. Pottery, dark brick-red
Height: 10 cm
Bronze Age, 19th century BC

One of the finest Bronze Age relics of the potter's craft, this vessel, shaped by hand without the use of a wheel, is almost perfectly symmetrical. The stamped ornament, alternating with bands which have been left blank, lends the surface a characteristic pattern-rhythm.

The tribes which left the Iberian Peninsula, passing along the valleys of the larger rivers to penetrate the interior of Europe, forming the most important wave of Western and Central European migration of the Bronze Age, were named after these vessels which are typical in shape and decoration. Reaching the Carpathian Basin, these mainly pastoral ethnic groups occupied only the tracts of land bordering the river Danube. At the final eastern point of their migration they formed settlements on and around the islets and flat lands by the river in the neighbourhood of present-day Budapest where, after a few decades of independent life, they became assimilated into the local farming and cattle-breeding inhabitants.

7 BRACELET

Site: Dunavecse, Bács-Kiskun County
Inv. No.: 72.5.1. Gold, hammered and engraved
Diameter: 7.7 cm
Bronze Age, 15th century BC

Acquired by purchase in 1972. The excavations carried out at Dunavecse yielded no information as to its origins.

The bracelet was cut by its maker from a gold plate 1.3 mm thick with a bronze chisel. The three encircling ribs, hammered into relief from the inside, divide the surface into four zones. Its decoration, formed by the combination of engraved straight lines, zigzags and star-shaped patterns, testifies to the aesthetic sensitivity of the goldsmith who made it.

In view of its size, shape and decoration, the Dunavecse bracelet must be regarded as a unique treasure. All the patterns decorating its surface were popular motifs among the goldsmiths working in the Carpathian Basin from the sixteenth to the fifteenth century BC. The bracelet, probably made in Transylvania, is likely to have reached the Danube region in the normal course of Bronze Age trade.

8 BRONZE HATCHET

Site: Mezőkomárom, Fejér County
Inv. No.: 74.5.1. Cast bronze
Length: 18.2 cm
Bronze Age, 15th century BC

During the sixteenth and fifteenth centuries BC the metal workshops of the Bronze Age Tisza peoples achieved one of their high peaks in the realms of craftsmanship. Among the popular jewellery and the weapons of the period their master craftsmen produced battle hatchets with tubular shafts which reached an outstanding artistic level. The hatchet found at Mezőkomárom is a fine example of this work; its graceful form follows the local tradition while its decoration, composed of sheaves of lines and rows of spirals, shows the influence of the neighbouring Aegean-Pontian states on the developing arts of the Bronze Age peoples in Hungary.

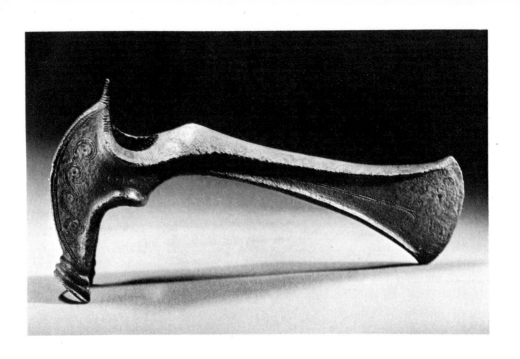

9 BRONZE BUCKET

Site: Hajdúböszörmény, Hajdú-Bihar County
Inv. No.: 33.1858.1. Bronze
Height: 31.5 cm
Late Bronze Age, 9th century BC

One of the most important relics of Bronze Age metal work in the Carpathian Basin was found on the confines of Hajdúböszörmény in 1858. The bronze treasures discovered here included vessels, swords and helmets. The most beautiful piece of the find was the bucket presented here. Its shoulder is covered with harmoniously composed decoration. The embossed horizontal rows of points flank bird-head-shaped motifs separated by round knobs. A circular ornament representing the sun, the symbol of ever reviving nature, stands out in the middle of the pattern.

In the prehistoric man's belief the picture of the bird represented life itself. The tenth to ninth centuries BC was the brightest period of the Tisza region's bronze industry whose products were much sought after even in distant countries.

10 URN

Site: Nagyberki, Somogy County
Inv. No.: 72.7.73. Pottery, black
Height: 75 cm
Early Iron Age, 7th century BC

The exploration of the earthworks and mounds at the site called Nagyberki-Szalacska had been already begun in the last century. New excavations were started in 1971 at which time the burial-chamber opened up in the first mound was found to contain two urns and some ashes. One of the urns, glistening with black graphite, published here, has been successfully restored. Its decoration consists of a horizontal groove running below the rim, together with ribs terminating in spirals on the broad neck of the urn and double spiral ribs which converge at certain points on the swelling shoulder.

The Szalacska urn ranks among the most beautiful specimens of the pottery of the Early Iron Age in Transdanubia.

The Szalacska earthwork towered above the valley of Kapos and thus controlled an important trade route. The deceased buried in the large mound with the urn—a masterpiece—must have been an important person in the community settled in the earthwork.

11 STAG-SHAPED SHIELD ORNAMENT

Site: Mezőkeresztes, Zöldhalompuszta, Borsod-Abaúj-Zemplén County
Inv. No.: 2/1929.1. Embossed plate, gold
Height: 37 cm
Second half of the 6th century BC

The find, which consisted of a gold stag, a gold chain decorated with lions, 136 hemispherical gold buttons and a pendant, was struck in 1928 at Zöldhalompuszta, an area belonging to Mezőkeresztes.

The embossed figure of the fallen stag is of gold. On its surface, between the horns and the neck, can be seen the head of a hook-billed bird. The eyes and ears are filled with pale blue glass-paste. Small rings for suspension are soldered to the reverse. Because the finders cut the figure of the stag in two, a triangular piece is missing from the middle. The object served originally as a shield ornament which may have been worn by a princely chieftain as a symbol of power.

Parallel pieces to the Zöldhalompuszta gold stag can be found among the remains from the tumuli of Scythian princes, discovered in the steppes at Kostromskaia, Kul-Oba.

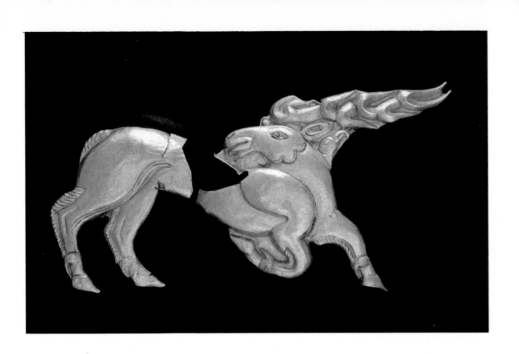

12 BRONZE RATTLES

Site: Nagytarcsa, Pest County
Inv. No.: 67.7.1–3. Cast bronze
Length: 23.1; 22.2; 17 cm
Beginning of the 5th century BC

In the course of a house building conducted in the village of Nagytarcsa in 1964 have come to light three bronze rattles, eight cattle-bells and two iron-bits.

Among these the most outstanding are the rattles, of which the tubular lower part was designed to hold a handle; the conical body is pierced by triangular holes. Each of two of the rattles is surmounted by a finely modelled stag—the top of the third is missing. Small iron balls inside the conical body make a rattling noise when the rattle is shaken.

Bronze rattles decorated with animals are characteristic of the Scythian Culture, a large number of them have been found in the tumuli on the steppes. The Nagytarcsa rattles can be used together with cattle-bells to produce a musical harmony. They did not serve as grave-goods, so their hiding seems to point to the probability that they formed a part of some cult or magical rite.

13 VESSEL WITH HANDLES DECORATED WITH HEADS OF BULLS
Site: Kósd, Nógrád County
Inv. No.: 46.1951.409. Fired clay, grey
Height: 18.5 cm
Celtic Age, 3rd century BC

The vessel found in the cemetery at Kósd is typical of the pots produced in series by Celtic potters using the method of throwing on the wheel. It is the expressive bulls' heads, forming the handles of this jar, which entitle it to an important place among the more precious relics of Celtic art.

The decoration of Celtic funerary vessels—mainly with the heads of bulls but occasionally with the heads of rams—probably had its roots in local traditions deriving from the representational art of the people inhabiting the Transdanubian regions in the early Iron Age, before the conquest of the Celts.

14 GOLD BEADS DECORATED WITH MASKS

Site: Szárazd-Regöly, Tolna County
Inv. No.: 67/1890 and 17/1891. Hammered gold plate
Diameter: 2.5–3.5 cm
Celtic Age, 2nd to 1st century BC

The beads are made up of two hemispheres of hammered gold foil joined by cords of twisted gold wire and, on some specimens, a ribbed band. The design on both hemispheres is almost identical; its main features are four human masks, arranged symmetrical-y in a square, separated by four large bosses. Superimposed on these are small elements composed of gold granules and twisted wire; each mask has a twisted wire fillet and the bosses are virtually transformed into pyramids by similar embellishments of wire and tiny spheres. These, too, are used to fill in the spaces between the larger features and are formed into spirals and small groups of granules symmetrically spaced.

The seven beads, with their decoration of masks, were found at the end of the last century as lot of the Szárazd-Regöly treasure I. The find included other types of gold beads whose ornaments, especially attached masks, are characteristic of the plastic style in Celtic art of the 3rd to the beginning of the 1st century BC. They were probably produced by goldsmiths of the South Transdanubian Celtic workshops.

15 BRONZE STATUE OF VICTORY

Site: Akasztó, Bács-Kiskun County
Inv. No.: 65.4.1. Cast bronze
Height: 18.6 cm
Roman Period, 1st century AD

Bronze statue representing Victory, the goddess of military triumph. Discovered in 1965 at Döbrögecpuszta, near the village of Akasztó, in the area bounded by the Danube and the Tisza.

The cast bronze figurine shows the goddess standing on a globe, with wings spread, holding in her hands the symbols of victory: a wreath and palm branch, these latter, however, not cast in one with the figures, are missing.

The site of the discovery is on the right bank of the Danube, 22 kilometres east of the river on the dwellings of the Sarmatians, opposite the Roman fortress at Dunakömlőd in Lussonium. Presumably the Sarmatians seized the statue on the occasion of one of their invasions into the territory of the Empire. The statue is to be dated at latest to the reign of the Emperor Tiberius (AD 14–37).

16 BRONZE LAMP DECORATED WITH A BUST OF JUPITER

Site: Mór, Fejér County
Inv. No.: 78.1913. Cast bronze
Height: 20.8 cm
Roman Period, 1st to 2nd century

The nozzle of the large bronze lamp is decorated with a beading and many-petalled flowers standing out in relief. A small suspension hook, made of a bent sheet, is riveted to the crescent-shaped reflector. The horns of the moon flank a splendidly modelled bust of Jupiter, while to the centre of the crescent, supported by a bunch of acanthus leaves, a smaller bust representing the sun-god Sol is soldered. Originally two small busts had been attached to the crescent, their position is still visible, but one of them must have got lost as far back as the Roman Period for it was then that the remaining bust was moved to its present central position. The eyes in both cases are inlaid. The unusually large bronze lamp made with excellent craftsmanship is covered by a fine, pale *verd-antique*. This valuable piece from the early imperial period, imported from Italy, belonged probably to a domestic altar in a wealthy Pannonian household.

17 VERIUCA'S TOMBSTONE

Site: Dunaújváros (Intercisa), Fejér County
Inv. No.: 56.1911.3. Limestone
Height: 149 cm; thickness: 16 cm; width: 87.6 cm
Roman Period, beginning of the 2nd century

Excavated in 1911 from a Roman tomb. The stone-carver represented the deceased woman in characteristic Eraviscan attire; she is shown wearing a kerchief over the head and her long-sleeved dress is fastened with a winged brooch on each shoulder. Her neck is encircled by two rows of a braided necklace with a round *bulla*, on her breast is a small pin. In her right hand she holds a spindle, in her left a type of distaff.

The two upper corners of the field are ornamented with acanthus leaves each bound by a rosette. Framed by a plain lath the inscription reads as follows: VERIVCA DA|NVI FILIA AN(norum)| XXX H(ic) S(ita) EST.|FLORVS EGRETA|RI F(ilius) CONIVGI | PIAE(ntissimae) T(itulum) M(emoriae) P(osuit). (Here rests Veriuca, daughter of Danuvius, aged thirty. The tombstone was erected in memory of the most pious wife of Florus, son of Egretarius.)

Both the tympanum and the lower part of the tombstone are broken. The names in the text preserve the usage of naming among the Celtic Eravisci.

18 PAIR OF SILVER BROOCHES

Site: Pátka, Fejér County
Inv. No.: 50.1897.1 and 4.1884. Silver with gold foil and cornelian decoration
Length: 15.4 cm
Roman Period, first half of the 2nd century

The pair of silver brooches we see here was a part of a woman's attire and probably came from one of the Pátka tumuli of the imperial period. One of the pair was brought to the surface by a farmer ploughing the ground, the other was purchased by the museum from a dealer in antiques five years later. This type of brooches have been named Norican-Pannonian after the area of diffusion, or 'winged fibulae' on account of their characteristic form. The flat bow and the catch-plate are covered with small gold lames bordered by filigree wire and decorated with spirals. The middle of the catch-plate of an elaborate open-work design is decorated by a square gold sheet with an oval cornelian.

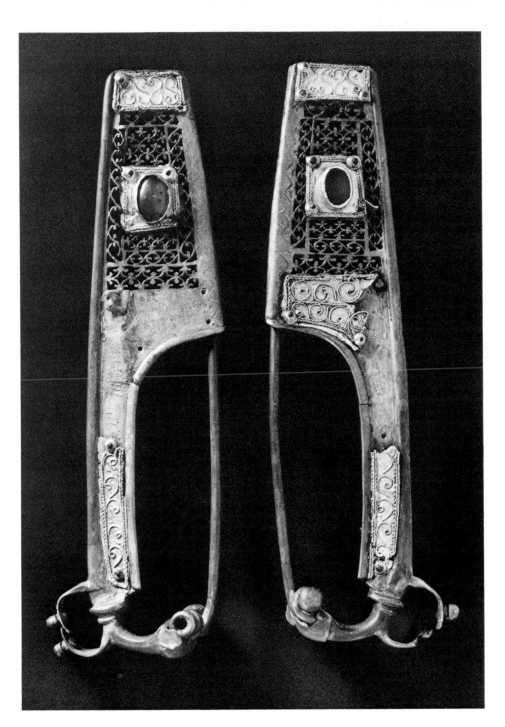

19 TERRA SIGILLATA VASE

Site: Tác, Fejér County
Inv. No.: 4.1937.5. Fired clay
Height: 16.6 cm
Roman Period, 2nd century

The short-necked, narrow-rimmed, globular vase stands on a comparatively small but well-shaped foot. The area decorated in relief is framed by beading at the top and a groove at the bottom. The whole vase is coated with a dull red glaze. The design was applied in the so-called barbotine technique. Among the heart-shaped leaves of the foliage a deer, its head turned backwards, is chased by a greyhound. This exquisitely stylized hunting scene is characteristic of the patterns of a Rhenish pottery manufacture (Rheinzabern), producing fine ceramics. This vase found its way to Pannonia via the Rhine-Danube waterways.

20 MODEL OF A GATEWAY

Site: Dunapentele (Intercisa), Fejér County
Inv. No.: 66.1906.352. Fired clay
Height: 31 cm
Roman Period, 2nd–3rd century

The model of a gateway has survived in a fragmentary condition, with only two stories preserved. It is flanked by two towers, pierced with windows and square in front but rounded at the back. Above the triple-arched door between the towers runs a frieze of lozenges. On the first floor, above the door, is a *tabula ansata* on which is incised, before firing, an inscription in cursive letters, which reads: (h)ILARVS FEC(it) PORTA(m) FEL(iciter).

The second storey has four windows beneath semicircular arches. Only the middle part of the top of the gate has survived. The third storey of the towers and their helm roofs—the latter probably pyramidal in shape and decorated with tracery—are missing. The floors and the towers are framed-in by heavy, impressed clay laths. The object is a model either of one of the Aquincum gates or of the Intercisa fortress entrance.

21 JUPITER DOLICHENUS PLAQUE

Site: Dunakömlőd, Bottyán mound, Tolna County
Inv. No.: 10.1951.106. Bronze plate coated with white metal
Height: 36.2 cm; width: 27.5 cm
Roman Period, early 3rd century

The triangular plaque belonging to the Jupiter Dolichenus cult was found at the site of the Dunakömlőd Roman fortress (Lussonium). In the centre is the usual representation of Jupiter Dolichenus: the god wearing a breastplate, scale armour and a round cap is shown standing on the back of a bull. He holds a thunderbolt in his left hand and a double axe in his right. The bull stands on a low base which bears the inscription: IOVI DVLCHENO P(ublius) AEL(ius) | LVCILIVS | > COH(ortis) I ALP(inorum) EQ(uitatae). (To Jupiter Dolichenus, Publius Aelius Lucilius, centurion of the 1st mounted Alpine cohort). On the upper part of the plaque, between two lines of dotted ornament, are half-length figures of Sol and Luna; next to Jupiter is seen a relief of Victory. The figure in the lower left corner represents Hercules with his club, in the right-hand corner is Minerva. The plaque was fastened to a staff and used as an ensign or *signum* on the occasion for religious rites.

22 FONDO D'ORO

Site: Dunaújváros (Intercisa), Fejér County
Inv. No.: 63.5.1. Glass
Diameter: 8.2 cm
Roman Period, end of the 4th century

The gold foil decoration *(fondo d'oro)*, sealed into the double glass bottom of the goblet, represents a married couple with their child. Judging from their clothing, the family must have belonged to the upper classes; the man was probably a high-ranking official at the imperial court.

According to its inscription the goblet belongs to the early Christian relics. Magnificent glass vessels of this kind were made in Rome, their Christian character emphasized sometimes also by inscriptions. Only two such specimens have been found in Pannonia. It may be presumed that glass vessels decorated with gold leaf were given as presents on family occasions—weddings or the birth or christening of a child, for instance—and were probably produced as individual pieces, specially commissioned to mark the event.

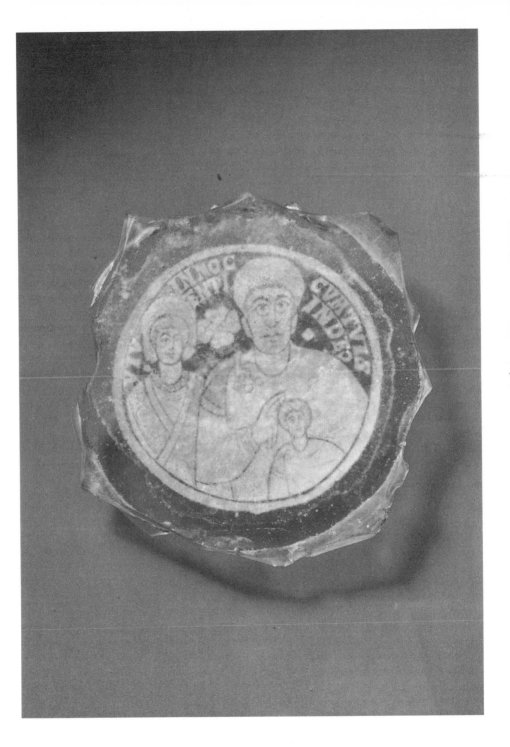

23 BRONZE CASKET MOUNTS

Site: Kisárpás, Győr-Sopron County
Inv. No.: 14.1927.1. Bronze, repoussé
Length: 30.5 cm; width: 8.8 cm
Roman Period, 4th century

The small pearwood casket, covered with bronze sheets in repoussé work, was found in a late Roman sarcophagus. Judging by the size of the sheets and the wooden parts which survive, the casket was probably about 31.5×28 cm in size. The part of the sheet which is in the best state of preservation, now coated with a bright *verd-antique* layer, is divided into four more or less square fields.

In the first field a maenad, wearing a dress hanging down in deep folds, steps briskly forward to threaten a child satyr, brandishing a rod in her right hand while with her left she seizes the boy's head. The two figures in the second field are separated from each other by a vase with ribbed decoration, standing on a column. A satyr, stepping forward on the left, reaches across the column to hand a bunch of grapes to Dionysus, a graceful figure on the right. The god, who rests his head on his right arm holds his emblem, a thyrsos, surmounted by a bunch of grapes in his left hand. His head is wreathed with a garland of grapes and ivy leaves. In the third field a small satyr, looking back with a scared expression on his face, is separated by a vine tendril from the bearded figure of Silenus who, holding a large jar in his left hand, proceeds solemnly towards the right. In the fourth field a beautifully proportioned Mars, holding in his right hand a spear and in his left a lowered shield, turns his helmeted head towards the naked Venus, stepping out to the right. The flowing hair of the goddess is fastened in the centre of her forehead with an ornament studded with precious stones; with lifted arms she gracefully arranges her veil on her head.

24 BUST OF VALENTINIAN II

Site: Pécs, Baranya County
Inv. No.: 108.1912.66. Bronze-gilt
Height: 12.2 cm
Roman Period, AD 375–392

The bust of the Emperor is framed by a laurel wreath. Seen from the front, the head is oval-shaped with regular features. The sleek hair, cut straight across the front, covers almost the whole of the brow. The diadem, consisting of a double row of beading, is ornamented with a jewel set in a square mount worn in the centre of the forehead. A folded cloak, fastened with a brooch, covers the chest and a part of the neck. The large brooch is ornamented with a knob at each corner. The lower part of the bust is damaged and the gilding is partly lost.

On the basis of its stylistic and iconographic characteristics, specialists have identified the bust as that of Valentinian II (375–392), though it was believed earlier to have represented the Emperor Constans. The destination for which the bust was intended has not been satisfactorily determined. It was formerly thought to have served as a decoration inside a dish presented as a gift by the emperor but according to more recent theories it may have been fixed to an inscribed bronze board containing a decree or an imperial deed of gift.

25 ORNAMENTAL BROOCH

Site: Szilágysomlyó (Şimleul-Silvaniei), Rumania
Inv. No.: 122/1895. 1. Gold and semi-precious stones
Length: 17.1 cm
Late antique, end of the 4th century

This splendid jewel is a part of the treasure found in 1899 in the course of agricultural work. A gold relic of similar age, now preserved in the Kunsthistorisches Museum, Vienna, has already been discovered on the same site as long ago as 1797.

The normal bow of the brooch is here substituted by an oval-shaped gold plate mounted with a meticulously polished black onyx. The eight circular cells embedded in a band which runs round the central onyx are set with red almandine; the whole is framed with a band of cloisonné work: small rectangles set with red garnets and white and green glass. The part which supports the bulbous knobs is decorated with large oval-shaped almandines and hemispherical rock-crystals.

Brooches with three pendants formed a part of the official imperial habit. From the fourth century onwards some of these were given to barbarian vassal kings in recognition of merit.

The treasure discovered at Szilágysomlyó which comprises lot II included ten pairs of gold brooches of various shapes and sizes, one large gold ring and three gold cups as well as the brooch seen here.

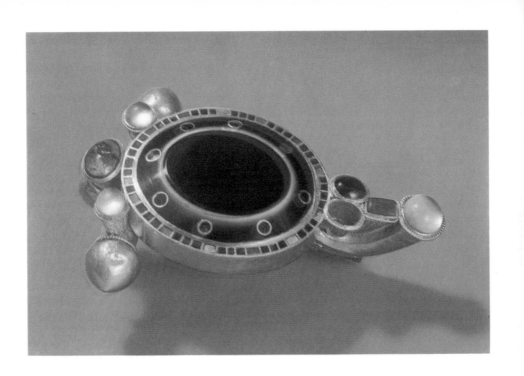

26 CEREMONIAL CAULDRON

Site: Törtel, Pest County
Inv. No.: 22.1869.1. Cast bronze
Height: 88 cm
Migration Period, first half of the 5th century

The cauldron was cast in bronze, and the casting seams visible on the surface indicate the use of a mould made up of four parts. The foot is missing but according to other similar specimens found in Hungary, Rumania and the Soviet Union, it was probably shaped as a truncated cone. The cauldron's decoration, showing raised ribs, is governed by the four areas into which it is divided.

Cylindrical cauldrons with handles similar to those of the Törtel specimen can be traced as having spread from the river Don to Central Europe; their appearance can be connected with the advance of the Huns which started at the end of the fourth century.

Cauldrons were probably used in fertility or other cultic rites. This presumption is corroborated by the scenes represented in rock-carvings found in Southern Siberia.

27 CORONET

Site: Csorna, Győr-Sopron County
Inv. No.: 55.36.1. Gold and semi-precious stones
Length: 27.6 cm
Migration Period, first half of the 5th century

The coronet was found in 1887, in a grave lying in a north–south position, fitted to a skull. The rest of the objects discovered are not in the Museum.

The piece is badly damaged. The gold plate, which slightly narrows towards the ends, was originally fixed to a bronze plate. The centre of the front is decorated with a large oval cornelian; the round cells are set with garnets, the triangular and lozenge-shaped cells with garnets, here and there with green glass. The coronet is characteristic of a kind of goldsmiths' work which relies for its effect on the ornamental use of coloured stones, a style that can be traced back to Sarmatian taste.

Gold coronets set with gems were worn by the wives of Alan and Hun leaders in the fourth and fifth centuries. They probably used them to hold in place their veils which, from evidence in finds, were richly ornamented with gold spangles.

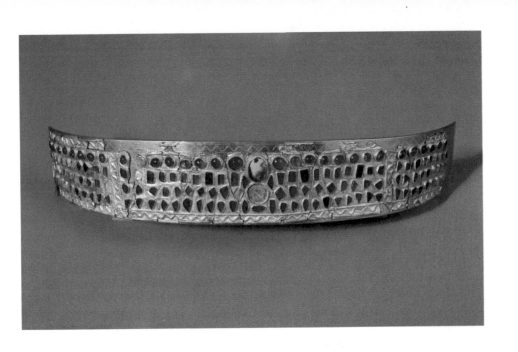

28 CICADA-SHAPED BROOCHES

Site: Györköny, Tolna County
Inv. No.: Orn. Jank. 48. Gold set with almandines
Length: 6.4 cm
Migration Period, first half of the 5th century

The two cicada-shaped brooches were purchased by the Hungarian National Museum from the Jankovich Collection.

Gold plate, set with almandines, is mounted on a cast silver base. The cells on the wings and head are surrounded by fine beaded wire, and the same type of wire frames the whole brooch and articulates the body of the cicada. The neck and the body are formed of grooved wire of various designs. Rows of dots designed to imitate granulation are produced by beating the gold plate from the back.

The cicada was widely believed to be a symbol of luck by the inhabitants of the ancient world. Asian Huns and the Chinese wore cicada-shaped ornaments pinned to their headdresses as a mark of rank. The brooches found at Györköny are typical of the jewellery produced in the Pontus region.

29 BRACELETS

Site: Dunapataj, Bakodpuszta, Bács-Kiskun County
Inv. No.: 19/1860.1. Gold set with almandines
Diameter: 8.5 cm
Migration Period, first half of the 5th century

In 1859 three graves containing the remains of richly bejewelled women were found at Bakodpuszta, near Dunapataj. In two of them, situated next to each other, a considerable quantity of gold jewellery was found. The richer of the two graves contained a gold necklace set with precious stones, a gold buckle, earrings, rings and gold spangles for veils, besides the two magnificent bracelets decorated with animal heads we see here.

The bracelets, embellished with confronted maned animal heads, are jointed so that they can be opened; the fastening is secured with a left-handed screw. On the animal heads the shapes of the nose, eyes, eyebrows, ears and collar are emphasized by dark red highly polished almandines set in heightened mounts.

The Bakodpuszta bracelets are masterpieces of the art of goldsmiths in the Black Sea region, which preserved the traditions of Hellenistic art.

More recent research points to the possibility that the Bakodpuszta site was the burial place of the family of Aedico, Prince of the tribe of Scyrri and a man in Attila's confidence. The jewelled woman may have been Aedico's wife, mother of Odoacer who drove the last Roman Emperor of the West from his throne.

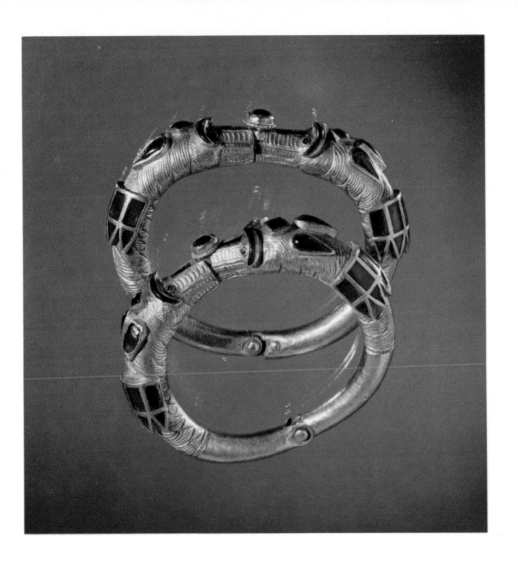

30 BROOCHES

Site: Szentendre, Pest County
Inv. No.: 66.1.228. Silver-gilt
Length: 8.8 cm, width: 5.8 cm
Migration Period, first half of the 6th century

The brooches, discovered in grave 56 of the Lombard cemetery excavated at Szentendre, are outstanding examples of the Pannonian Lombard style. What can be called the head-plate and the foot-plate are both richly decorated. The semicircular fan-like part with projecting knobs includes motifs of the Germanic animal style, while the oval section terminates in an animal head with interlace ornament.

Pannonia came under the rule of the Lombards in AD 526. Their reign lasted about four decades. By 568 Alboin and his people had already moved to Italy. The brooches discovered at Szentendre may have been made in a goldsmith's workshop producing the popular type of jewellery of the period. The fact that similar brooches having semicircular head-plates decorated with seven to nine knobs have survived in Italian Lombard assemblages, such as those of Ravenna and Testona, is an indication of the living traditions of Pannonian workshops.

Numerous excavations, among them that of grave 56 in Szentendre cemetery, corroborate the fact that brooches usually occur in pairs.

31 DISK-SHAPED BROOCH

Site: Keszthely, Fenékpuszta, Veszprém County
Inv. No.: 61.72.1. Moulded silver
Diameter: 4.7 cm, height: 0.8 cm
Migration Period, 6th century

The round central plaque is ornamented with a figural design—a mounted warrior killing a dragon. This is surrounded by a scalloped border. The scene of the warrior closely resembles the Roman favourite pattern appearing among others as decoration of bronze casket-mounts. Iconographically the figure on horseback represents a saint and derives from the image of the fight between Chimaera and Bellerophon in works of classical antiquity.

The brooch was excavated at Fenékpuszta in the last century. It was found outside the southern wall of the late Roman originally fortified settlement where, in addition to Roman graves, sixth century cemeteries were found too. The specimen to which this disc brooch is most closely related also comes from a sixth century cemetery at Fenékpuszta, it was discovered in a grave excavated near the *horreum* situated inside the walls. The two brooches are clearly products of the same workshop. The traditions and date of the type to which these brooches belong cannot be considered to have been definitely identified up to now. Direct Byzantine influence may have played a part in their creation as well as Roman inheritance still survived.

32 CRESCENT-SHAPED EARRING

Provenance unknown
Inv. No.: Orn. Jank. No. 23. Gold
Height: 5 cm
Migration Period, 7th century

"In the centre a heart-shaped ornament is supported by foliage. The heart itself is decorated with three punched dots. Above this is a double leaf and a group of three leaves. On each of the two sides the space is filled by a peacock. On the lower rim seven balls were added." (Gy. László).

Similar earrings from the Carpathian Basin are known; they come from the graves of women of distinguished families buried in cemeteries of the Avar Period. Judging by the territory in which similar jewels have been found, it can be assumed that they were actually produced in the Byzantine Empire and from there had become wide-spread in neighbouring countries. The Byzantine state paid regular taxes to the early Avars. The earring may have been paid as a part of such a tax or, alternatively, it may have been bought by the Avars with the proceeds of this revenue.

33 EARRINGS

Site: Szentendre, Pest County
Inv. No.: 228/1871.II.1. Gold
Length: 5.5 cm
Migration Period, beginning of the 7th century

The exact circumstances of the discovery of these earrings are not known. Judging by other objects which found their way with them to the museum they may have come from a grave in which a man and two women were buried. In view of the splendour of the assemblage of finds the family grave is classified as the burial place of a chieftain.

Some of the finds, such as a reed-leaf shaped spearhead and two stirrups with oblong-shaped loops, as well as two earrings of small size were probably found next to the male skeleton. Close parallels to the weapon and the type of horse equipment can be found among South Siberian and North Mongolian antiquities. In Hungary these objects are typical of the group of finds connected with the first Avar invasion. Gold coins belonging to the grave-goods, issues of Justinus II (AD 565–578) and Phokas (AD 602–610) with oblong-shaped loops, help us to date the finds.

The earrings are of excellent workmanship. Surviving cells surrounded by a framework of globules suggest inlaid decoration for the pyramid-shaped pendant. Both the globules of the framework and the much larger gold bead at the tip of the pyramid are hollow. Gold earrings of this type are an indication of the trade relations which must have existed between the Avars and the inhabitants of the Pontus region in the sixth and seventh centuries.

34 NECKLACE

Site: Kiskőrös, Vágóhíd-dűlő, Bács-Kiskun County
Inv. No.: 12/1935, 2–6. Gold set with almandines
Length: 1.8 cm, almandine pendants: 3.6 × 1.7 cm to 4.4 × 2.7 cm
Migration Period, 7th century

This jewel comes from Grave 'A', a little girl's grave, in the early Avar cemetery excavated at the outskirts of Kiskőrös. It may originally have been part of a decorated collar made-up of ornaments of various kinds. Jewellery of this type followed the fashions set by the Byzantine court. Other objects found in the same grave confirm the fact that this five or six-year-old girl was a member of an aristocratic family.

The collar, of interwoven gold wire, is hung with pendants shaped as truncated cones, reminiscent of little bells, and five almandines of different sizes. These polished egg-shaped stones, convex on the face and concave at the back, are, with one exception, attached by grooved gold bands to the framing. In the centre, at the point where the gold bands meet, these pendants are inlaid with blue glass paste.

According to Gyula László, the burial of members of the princely family at Kiskőrös may have started in the 650s; the head of the clan was buried at Bócsa.

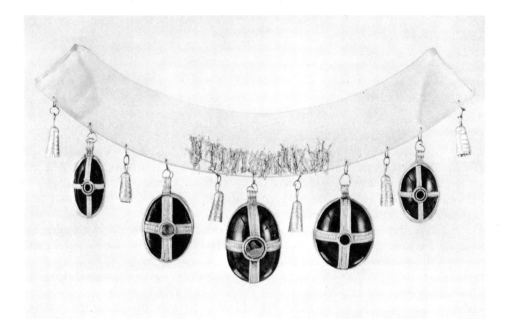

35 STRAP-END

Site: Kiskőrös, Vágóhíd-dűlő, Bács-Kiskun County
Inv. No.: 4/1935.3. Silver repoussé, engraved
Length: 9 cm
Migration Period, 7th century

The strap-end was found in Grave 9 of the burial ground of a princely Avar family during the excavations at Kiskőrös. Most of the graves had already been disturbed and robbed during the Avar Period. Shreds of gold with a woven pattern left in the grave are an indication of the former riches of the deceased occupant.

The large silver strap-end we see here consists of two plates, both decorated with engraved palmettes against a punched background.

The strap-end found at Kiskőrös is one of the earliest specimens on which palmettes set against a punched background occur—a characteristic pattern of eighth and ninth century belt ornaments cast in bronze.

36 BELT ORNAMENTS

Site: Bócsa, Bács-Kiskun County
Inv. No.: 7.1935.2.4. Gold with inlaid glass
Length: 4.5 cm, width: 2.6, 2.2 cm
Migration Period, 7th century

According to Gyula László's reconstruction the gold belt ornaments, found in 1935 in a princely grave at Bócsa, belonged originally to two belts, one of which was decorated with pseudo-buckles. The prince's quiver, his gold-mounted drinking horn and his dagger were suspended from this belt as he probably wore them when he was alive.

In addition to six pseudo-buckles, a similar number of different kinds of belt ornaments, two belt-holeguards, three small strap-ends and a large strap-end belonging to the set described above were also found. A common characteristic is that they are all set with stones and all decorated with outlines in beading. In the centre of both the pseudo-buckles and the oval mounts the larger cells are inlaid with pale greenish glass, while the cells of the second belt are filled with small flat garnets. The mounts were fastened to the belts by means of hooks fixed to the reverse side. The fashion for belts decorated with pseudo-buckles is a manifestation of the Byzantine influence to which the industrial arts of the Black Sea region, based on ancient tradition, were subject.

37 LARGE STRAP-END AND BELT ORNAMENTS

Site: Kecel, Bács-Kiskun County
Inv. No.: 7/1933. 30.33. Gilded cast bronze
Length: 11.5 cm, width: 3 cm, 3.2 cm
Migration Period, 8th century

These objects belong to a belt-set cast in bronze, found in Grave 32 of the late Avar Period cemetery excavated at Kecel-Határdűlő. The large strap-end with a beaded border is ornamented with a scene of fighting animals. In the middle a winged griffin presses its claws into the back leg of a hind which has sunk to its knees. The wounded animal turns his head back towards his attacker. Facing the hind is a leaping lion with a man's face. The other ornaments, six open-work mounts decorated with griffins, were cast in the same mould.

Both fighting beasts and griffins were popular motifs of the so-called 'griffin-tendril' group produced during the late Avar Period (after AD 670).

Searches for a provenance for these ornamental motifs have revealed connections which can be traced back through south Russian Greek-Scythian material to Central Asia.

Date of foundation:	1951
Collections:	Objects from the Conquest Period of the Magyars
	Medieval archaeological remains from
	the Age of the Árpád dynasty
	the Middle Ages
	the period of the Turkish occupation
	Lapidarium
	Goldsmiths' work
	Bells
Number of items:	60,410

MEDIEVAL HISTORY DEPARTMENT

From the Museum's early collection of basic material, acquired between 1802 and 1844, 9,641 items have come to this Department. In the collection of goldsmith's work as well as among the remains from the age of the Magyar Conquest we find here many pieces of outstanding interest, also by European standards, as e.g. the Monomachos crown and a number of sabretache plates.

Since its formation the Department's collection has been increased by not only newly excavated material, but also by a number of outstanding works of art bought by the Museum, as, for instance, the Nádasdy cup, a Turkish leather mantle, etc. In 1967 the funerary crowns of Béla III and his wife were transferred to the Hungarian National Museum from the Matthias Church of Buda Castle.

The Department's scientific work is divided among several research programmes. Study of the cemeteries dating from the Magyar Conquest has uncovered many new facts concerning the social structure, daily life and customs of the Magyar people. One of its major undertakings is research into 'Centres of Officialdom [known as *ispánság*] and the Seats of the Chieftains of the Clans'.

Led by István Méri, research by the team of archaeologists examining medieval villages has produced some significant results.

Under the heading 'Research on Feudal Centres'—the earliest period of the foundation of the Hungarian state—the exploration of the princely and subsequent royal courts at Esztergom yielded significant results. A quantity of historical data and much information of architectural and cultural interest was also obtained in the course of excavations in other feudal centres as well as on the sites of castles and monasteries.

Researches into the development of goldsmiths' work in Hungary aim at elaborating a comprehensive catalogue of the Museum's large collection. A further important objective is the investigation of remains of Turkish craftsmanship practised in Hungary.

The Department played a part in the staging of the 1967 exhibition entitled "Hungary's History from the Magyar Conquest to 1849" as well as in a number of temporary exhibitions both at home and abroad.

Emese Nagy

38 SABRETACHE PLATE

Site: Szolyva (Svaliava), Soviet Union
Inv. No.: 148/1870.5. KKO. Silver plate with richly gilded background
Height: 12.5 cm, length: 11.3 cm
Magyar Conquest, 10th century

Drawn two-dimensionally and left in the natural silver of which the plate is made, bouquets of palmettes in a continuing pattern stand out conspicuously against the gilded background. The upper border is decorated with a row of tassel-shaped mounts.

Distinguished members of clans and leaders of their military escorts wore the ornamental belts designed to carry their sabres as symbols of their status. A leather bag, either inlaid or ornamented with tooled patterns, held the flint and steel and whetstone which was an essential part of their military equipment and this too hung from the belt. As time went on, the leather bag became a decorative as well as a useful accessory, first by covering with metal plates the area round the fastening of the flap and by elaborating the strap with which it was fastened with metal mounts. Following these, cast ornaments were fitted round the border of the flap and to the bag beneath it. Gradually, rivalling each other in magnificence, the wearers applied bigger and bigger mounts and plates until these decorations lost their original functional structure and covered the whole surface of the sabretache. At this point it obviously became more practical to cover it entirely with a single silver plate which could be elaborately ornamented with goldsmiths' work before it was attached to the basic leather bag.

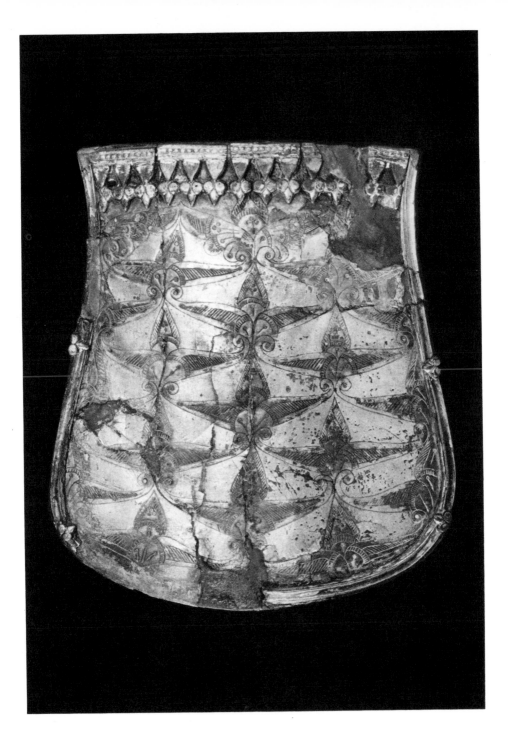

39 APEX OF TALL FUR CAP

Site: Beregszász (Beregovo), Soviet Union
Inv. No.: 51/1900. 20–21. KKO. Gilded silver plate
Height: originally about 12.5 cm
Magyar Conquest, 10th century

The pattern was carried out on a flat silver plate before it was moulded into its present cone-shape and, finally, the two indented edges were joined by soldering. The knob on the top, made up of two half-spheres, was soldered on separately. The pattern itself begins, close to the bottom of the cone, with four double palmettes from each of which two curled leaves, springing from a central stem, rise upwards until the whole of the tapering surface is covered by a trellis. In the interstices, formed by the bunches of leaves, palmettes growing from each other and decreasing in size, form three repeats. The surface pattern is terminated by an interlaced band running round the base of the knob which is, itself, decorated with circles and dots. Both the upper and the lower edges of the cone are surrounded with double twisted wires, soldered separately to the surface. Round the lower edge, at the base of the palmettes, are pairs of holes and at the point where the palmette-leaves meet, as well, making a total of twelve tiny holes decorating the cone. This silver cone from Beregszász must have glittered as a peak on the tall fur-trimmed leather or felt hat of some high-born Hungarian.

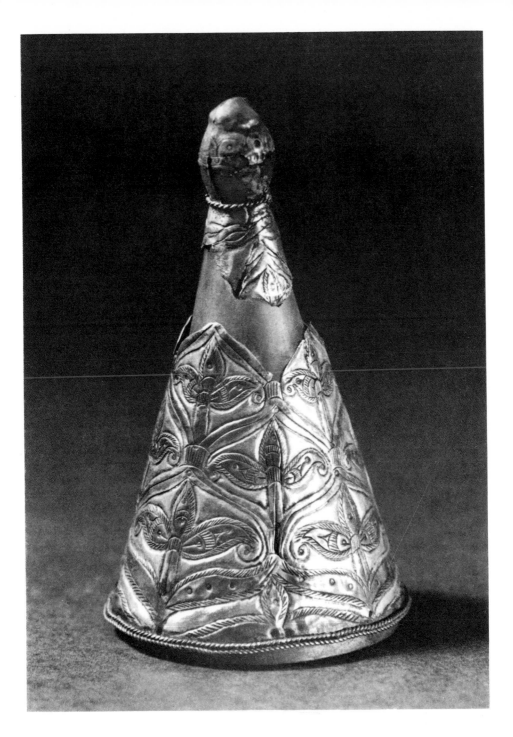

40 ORNAMENTS WORN IN PLAITS OF HAIR

Site: Tiszaeszlár, Bashalom, Szabolcs-Szatmár County
Inv. No.: 60.17.1.2, 5–6, 8–9 A. KKO. Cast silver, gilded
Diameter of metal disks: 5 cm, diameter of shell disks: 3.6 and 3.2 cm
Magyar Conquest, 10th century

Each of the two metal disks is bordered by a raised frame within which stands a stylized four-legged animal in front of a tree of life composed of floral elements. The tails and crests of the beasts merge into the foliage of the trees, their bodies are divided into sunk areas, which are gilded. Under the belly can be seen the trunks of the trees, which divide as they rise up. A bronze plate is riveted to the back of these open-work disks and, judging from some minute traces of stuff, a coloured pad of felt or leather may have been inserted between the two plates to set off the pattern. In the supporting bronze plates are holes, two at the top for attaching the plate and two more, set much further apart, from which ornaments were hung. The straps which were used to suspend the disks were decorated with a row of mounts shaped as the heads of cows. In the case of one of the sets a lost mount was subsequently replaced by a lozenge-shaped button. The pair of disks made of polished shells from the river-bed, which have a mother-of-pearl lustre, hung beside the metal ones. They are pierced at the top and the bottom and from the lower hole a string of coloured beads was suspended. Recent study has proved beyond question that the longer end of the strap (it was decorated only along its shorter length) must have been worn plaited into the hair.

41 BITS AND STIRRUPS

Site: Muszka (Musca), Rumania
Inv. No.: 45/1898. 3–4, 9. KKO. Forged iron and inlaid silver
Length of bit: 30.5 cm, height of stirrup: 18.1 cm and 17.8 cm, width: 12.9 cm and 13.4 cm
Magyar Conquest, 10th century

The arches of the stirrups and those parts of the bits which lie outside the horse's mouth are decorated with inlaid silver in transverse stripes.

The conquering Magyars buried their horses with their dead as 'travelling companions' but only the skull and the leg-bones of the horse were left inside the skin. It was believed that from these parts alone the horse could be brought back to life. The remains of the horse were placed on the left side of the rider, that is to say on the side from which the horse was mounted, and the carcass of the horse was harnessed. Sometimes the collar and the bit were actually pulled into the horse's head and the saddle with the stirrups placed on its back. It faced the west, the direction in which it had to carry its rider to the realm of the dead.

There is little information available on the disturbed graves at Muszka but the decoration of the harness we see here and, in addition, the structure of the bit connected by four rings (which made it possible to control the horse more precisely) as well as the large size of the weighty stirrups point to the probability that the owner was a man of high rank.

42 THE MONOMACHOS CROWN

Site: Nyitraivánka (Ivanka pri Nitre), Czechoslovakia
Inv. No.: 1860.99.1-4; 1961. 37. 1–2; 1861.51. 1–2. KKO. Gold with cloisonné enamel
Height of the largest section: 11.5 cm
Between 1042 and 1050

The crown consists of seven slightly curved cloisonné enamelled gold plaques, rect-angular in shape but with arched tops. They are of various sizes and placed side by side in an upright position. The plaques were ploughed up and were delivered to the National Museum one by one. Its present diadem arrangement is based on analogous pieces, the reconstruction being governed by the size of the plaques and by the direction which the enamelled figures are facing. The central and tallest plaque represents Constantine Monomachos IX in his imperial robes and with his name inscribed round his head. It is flanked on either side by plaques of smaller size on which are the figures of the Empresses Theodora and Zoe. Next to these, of somewhat smaller size again, are two plaques on each of which is a female dancer; they represent Justice and Humility. The imperial figures and the dancers are surrounded by foliated scrolls in which are perched coloured birds. The plaques are of thin gold plate decorated with champlevé enamel. The excellent quality of the pictures of the imperial personages and the enamel work itself demonstrate beyond doubt that the crown was made in the workshop of the Byzantine Emperor's goldsmith. The portraits on the plaques enable the crown to be accurately dated: the joint reign of the Emperor Constantine Monomachos IX, his wife Zoe and her sister Theodora extended from 1042 to 1050.

Tradition has it that the crown was sent to Hungary by the Byzantine emperor as a present to King András I, who reigned from 1046 to 1061.

43 CLOISONNÉ ENAMEL RING

Site: Székesfehérvár, Fejér County
Inv. No.: 56.68.B. KKO. Cast gold, engraved and enamelled
Diameter: 2.3 cm, size of head: 1.2×1.3 cm
End of the 11th century

The hoop of the ring divides into two foliated scrolls which curl backwards with engraved double central ribs. The foliage in the shape of a V is attached to the round boss by a branch curved to a half circle with a similar rib. Two large globular buds are placed at each side at the point of juncture. The circular boss of the ring encloses the head of a queen, executed in flesh-coloured and white cloisonné enamel on a green background. Her Byzantine crown resembles the lower part of the Hungarian royal crown; its circular hoop is surmounted by a decorative crest; from the hoop hang pendants which reach the level of her cheek-bones.

44 PAIR OF CLOAK ORNAMENTS

Site: unknown
Inv. No.: 57.17.1–2.C. KKO. Silver-gilt
Diameter: 12 cm
Second half of the 13th century

The base of these two identical pieces of jewellery is an eight-foil round disk decorated round the border with pearls alternating with jewels. Today only three amethysts survive in each, the pearls are all missing. In the middle of each of the clasps, in a round filigree frame, is a double-headed eagle with spread wings. A large blue amethyst in an oval mount is set in its breast. The eagle displayed, as in heraldry, originally had eyes of pearl and a beak decorated with jewels.

The fact that the backs of these large pieces of jewellery show no trace of any fastening device and, furthermore, the presence of small holes round their edges, shows that they were sewn onto the garments they served to decorate. Contemporary works of art show that long mantles, which were a part of the dress of thirteenth-century aristocrats, were worn, decorated on the shoulder or, in pairs, on the chest with similar ornaments.

45 AQUAMANILE REPRESENTING A MOUNTED HUNTER

Site: Büngösdpuszta, Békés County
Inv. No.: 1885.99. KKO. Chased cast bronze
Height: 26 cm, length: 30 cm
Middle of the 12th century

This highly stylized horse, with large convex almond-shaped eyes and elongated cheeks, has a spout in its muzzle. The neck is thick, the chest broadened to give an impression of strength and the trunk broad and flat. The horse stands with its short legs apart; from its twisted tail only the stump has survived. On the right-hand side of the neck is a running hare, worked in relief while behind the saddle, on its rump, stands a small dog. The rider is seated in a saddle with high pommels, his helmet is missing and the nape of his neck shows signs of a break. He has a thick neck, a cylindrical body and flattened arms; his right arm, which is broken at the elbow, is slightly outstretched, while on his left he holds a long tapering shield. The garment he wears, a surcoat, is slit open at the front and at the back; it reaches to mid-calf on each side of the saddle, without folds. On his feet, which are set in the stirrups, he wears spurs with short spikes; the feet themselves are broken. The vessel was filled through the head of the rider. The Büngösdpuszta rider belongs to a small group of *aquamaniles*, of which six pieces are known. Three of them were found on the territory of medieval Hungary so it may be assumed that the mounted huntsman type of *aquamaniles* are of Hungarian origin.

46 CANDLESTICK IN THE FORM OF A SIREN

Site: Hajdúhadház, Monostor-dűlő, Hajdú-Bihar County
Inv. No.: 1892. 105. KKO. Cast bronze, originally gilded
Height: 20.5 cm, length: 15 cm
Second half of the 12th century

The female torso, with human legs, rises from the body of a bird. The long wings stretch backwards to rest on the ground. The broad body of the bird is decorated with a reticulate pattern while the engraving on its wings and tail suggests feathers. Resting on its back are foliated scrolls in tracery with arched tendrils. The end of one branch rests on the bird's tail, two more bend forward over the shoulders of the siren, their ends held in her uplifted scraggy arms. From the nape of her neck the candlestick itself rises out of small leaves, its tall spike is surrounded by a scalloped candle-drip.

Similar candlesticks were produced in fairly large numbers in Lorraine during the second half of the thirteenth century; the Hajdúhadház siren is of special interest because this richly decorated object of distinctive form was, in spite of belonging to costly imported goods, discovered on the site of a simple village church in Hungary.

47 DECORATIVE BASE OF A CROSS

Site: Szentmiklós, Komárom County
Inv. No.: 1870.25.2. KKO. Cast bronze, gilded and chased
Height: 15.1 cm, diameter: 12 cm
Second half of the 12th century

This exceptionally fine base of a cross—identical in structure to similar bases of Roman-esque candlesticks of the period—was found at the end of the last century in the Vértes Mountains, together with other ecclesiastical objects, hidden underground. The lower part forms a three-sided pyramid resting on three feet in the form of winged dragons. The openwork pattern of the sides is composed of arching three-ribbed scrolls ending in leaves opening fanwise. Winged dragons lurk in the curling branches and along the edge of each slope, above each foot, an intricately sculptured dragon creeps down. The node in the centre of the smooth cylindrical stem is decorated with scrolls and dragons, similar to those of the lower part; the upper part is a truncated pyramid, inverted. The sides, horizontally ribbed, are decorated with four motifs of open-work scrolls which protrude at the corners. The cross itself was inserted in the long opening at the top.

48 PROCESSIONAL CRUCIFIX

Site: Cegléd, Pest County
Inv. No.: 1904.79. KKO. Cast bronze, gilded
Height: 19.6 cm, width: 11.1 cm
Second half of the 12th century

The arms of the cross are modelled to resemble rough-hewn branches; at the ends of the horizontal arms are rhomboid tablets, inscribed: NAZ(AR ENV)S + ; the tablet, formerly at the top, is missing. Some of the letters of the inscription are engraved in reverse and on both tablets the second line of the inscription reads from right to left. The tablet at the top probably bore the name of Jesus. The upright limb of the cross rises from the sculptured head of a lion and on either side of the lion's mouth ornamental trifoliate scrolls form a heart-shaped curve towards the lower part of the cross's upright limb. Under the lion's head is the thick spike for attaching the crucifix to its staff.

The head of the image of Christ is bent a little forward and to the right. The hair, parted in the middle, falls onto the shoulders in parallel locks. Like the hair, the beard and moustache are engraved to give a formalized resemblance to hair. The eyes are closed; the arms sag at the elbow to suggest the weight of the hanging body; the palms of the hands are pierced through with large nails. The ribs of the torso are marked by engraved curved parallel lines. The loin-cloth is held by a broad belt and folds are indicated to show that it is tucked into the belt above the hips.

The crucifix of Cegléd was made before the Mongol invasion of Hungary in 1241–42 and is one of the most outstanding examples of the many processional crosses that have been preserved. The bent uncrowned head and slightly bent knees of the Cegléd figure are conceived with a fine sensitivity in their evocation of the dead Christ and place the crucifix among the best European works of the same type which were, by this period, widespread.

49 FUNERARY JEWELS OF BÉLA III AND ANNA OF ANTIOCH

Site: Székesfehérvár, Fejér County
Inv. No.: 1848.61.1–2, 1848.64.2.b–k. KKO
End of the 12th century

The mortal remains of King Béla III (1173–1196) and his first consort, Anna of Antioch (d. 1184), were enclosed in two undamaged and intact red marble sarcophagi found at the site of the ruins of the cathedral at Székesfehérvár, the church where once coronations and royal burials in Hungary took place. The burials were solemnized *regio more*, that is, the bodies of the royal couple were put in the grave accompanied by their royal insignia.

The tomb of Béla III contained a crown, a sword, a sceptre, a pair of spurs, a pectoral ornament, a bracelet and a processional cross, while that of his wife included a crown, a ring, a garment with gold lace decoration.

The gold RINGS from the grave (diameter: 3.5 cm and 2.5 cm) were personal jewels of the royal couple. The ring of Béla III is set with almandines and bears an inscription in Arabic. Below the stone is a tiny reliquary. The Queen's ring is set with an intaglio garnet showing a siren playing the lute.

The silver-gilt FUNERARY CROWNS are of the simplest shape (diameter: 19.7 cm and 18 cm). Their plain head-bands support four standing Greek crosses.

The PROCESSIONAL CROSS (height: 22.3 cm) is an ecclesiastical furnishing which ranks beside the bronze crucifixes surviving from the twelfth century; it bears the marks of repeated repairs. The ENKOLPION (height: 8 cm) was placed in the grave to substitute, as a symbol, a reliquary worn round the neck. It was suspended from a silver chain. The reliquary, produced in Byzantium in the eleventh century, was originally decorated on both sides with gold plates of cloisonné enamel. This object, damaged in the course of time, was placed in its present incomplete condition in the grave of Béla III; of the original ten plates only four survive.

The PAIR OF SPURS (length: 10.3 cm) belongs to the set of royal insignia. The plain broad BRACELET, consisting of a silver band (diameter: 8.4 cm) found on the king's right wrist again forms part of the insignia.

The SCEPTRE (height: 50.8 cm) is a bent rod of sheet-silver with a fleur-de-lis at the upper end. In design it corresponds to fleur-de-lis sceptres we know from contemporary works of art.

The SWORD, also cut from sheet-silver (length: 53 cm) is very simple, restricted in shape to a basic form.

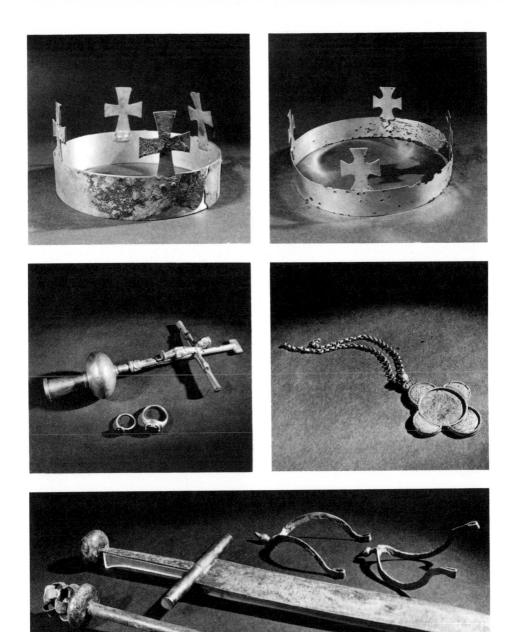

50 AQUAMANILE IN THE FORM OF A CENTAUR

Site: Abaújszántó, Borsod-Abaúj-Zemplén County
Inv. No.: 1860.115 KKO. Cast bronze, engraved, pounced and chased
Height: 42.5 cm
c. 1200

The centaur, who beats a drum and carries a child playing a flute on his back, has the body of a human being down to the waist. His sensitively drawn and finely modelled face is framed by hair tucked behind the ears and falling round his shoulders, the locks marked by incised parallel lines. The pupils of the eyes, now deeply indented, may once have been inlaid with some coloured substance. The long moustache curls upwards at the ends and the beard is tightly curled. The centaur holds a drum decorated with pierced holes, close to his chest; from the drum a protruding spout ends in a dragon's head. The centaur's right arm, bent forward from the elbow, is held close to the body, its hand may originally have held a drumstick. The other arm rests on the drum. The torso of the centaur is clothed in a garment covered with an incised design of vertical stripes consisting of parallel oblique lines. Below the waist the figure is developed into the form of a horse, its surface decorated with a regular pattern of circles, engraved with cross-hatching, and groups of four small dots arranged rhomboidally.

The provenance of this object is difficult to determine. It probably comes from the Rhine–Maas region, a centre of bronze-casting at this period, but it is also possible that it was the work of a Hungarian craftsman.

51 STONEWORK WITH CARVED DRAGON

Site: Pomáz, Klissza-dűlő, Pest County
Inv. No.: 60.17.1896.C. KKO. Sandstone
Height: 31 cm, length at the top: 81.5 cm, at the base: 51 cm, 31.5 cm thick
13th century

The stone is a building element, perhaps an *impost*, surrounded by smoothly cut planes, the top and base horizontal and the ends converging downwards. The face of the stone, an irregular trapezoid in shape, is decorated with a dragon carved in low relief. The roughly finished reverse suggests that the stone was set into a wall. The dragon is closely decorated with incised lines and a pattern simulating scales. It is surrounded on three sides by a plain carved band; the fourth side is damaged so that the carving is not complete. The head of the dragon, open-mouthed and sharp-toothed, is joined to its ovoid body by an S-shaped neck with a short mane. The beast has the legs and wings of a bird, covered with stylized feathers; its tail, curled into a loop, is carved in the same style as its neck.

According to the description of Sándor Sashegyi the carving was found during the excavation carried out in 1937–39 on the site of the chancel of a Gothic church. Remains of an earlier Romanesque church were found in the same village.

52 EARTHENWARE JAR

Site: Hatvan, Sugar-refinery, Heves County
Inv. No.: 20/1892.4. KKO. Yellowish-white fired clay, with brownish-red stripes
Height: 29.6 cm
13th century

According to inventory entries, the four earthenware jars which were donated to the Museum were found at a spot where there may formerly have been a well. Human skulls and bones were also discovered on the site of the Hatvan factory. These circumstances seem to point to the fact that the jars came originally from a settlement of the period of the Árpád dynasty.

The painted jar, with its slender shape, which we see here, is made of clay thinned down with sand and fine-grained grit. Its yellowish-white surface is somewhat rough to the touch. Its swelling ovoid belly, with a slightly rounded high shoulder, narrows sharply to a thin neck and ends in a broad rim which finally turns inwards. Surrounding the jar, where the neck meets this rim, is a very thin sharply projecting ridge. The jar is decorated with ten broad horizontal stripes, painted in brownish-red; a similar stripe runs round the inside of the rim.

53 VESSELS FROM ARPADIAN VILLAGES
11th to 13th centuries

EARTHENWARE CAULDRON
Site: Kardoskút, Békés County. István Méri's excavation, 1955
Inv. No.: 58.102.77.B. KKO. Fired clay
Height: 20.5 cm, diameter of mouth: 27.3 cm

Coloured dark brown with traces of red paint on the rim and the outside. The vessel is tall and broad; its straight sides widen from the top down. Two holes, by means of which the vessel could be hung up, have been pierced on opposite sides of the rim which thickens as it turns inward.

POT
Site: Kardoskút, Békés County
Inv. No.: 58.101.3.B. KKO. Fired clay
Height: 18.5 cm, diameter of mouth: 17.5 cm, diameter of base: 12.5 cm

Made on a potter's wheel. Dark brown in colour. A wide-mouthed, convex-shouldered stocky vessel. Below a rusticated ornamentation are three incised lines. On the base a mark in the form of a cross.

POT
Site: Bashalom, Szabolcs-Szatmár County
Inv. No.: 68.92.3.B. KKO. Fired clay
Height: 19 cm, diameter of mouth: 11.3 cm, diameter of base: 10.5 cm

Made on a potter's wheel. Light greyish-brown in colour. A narrow-necked, convex-shouldered, stocky vessel. The edge of its rim, which turns gently outwards, has a thin ridge attached to it. On the shoulder is a rusticated ornament, below which the whole body is decorated with incised spirals. On the base a mark in the form of a cross.

DISH
Site: Bashalom, Szabolcs-Szatmár County
Inv. No.: 68.92.2.B. KKO. Fired clay
Height: 9.6 cm, diameter of mouth: 16–17 cm, diameter of base: 8 cm

Made on a potter's wheel. Pale greyish-brown in colour, a wide-mouthed, convex-bellied vessel narrowing downwards. The edge of its rim is angular. Marked on the base with a Maltese cross.

The vessels shown here are characteristic pieces from a set of eleventh to thirteenth century village kitchen utensils.

54 FINGER-BOWL

Site: Bátmonostor, Bács-Kiskun County
Inv. No.: App. Jank. 186. KKO. Beaten copper, gilt, engraved, chased and enamelled
Height: 3.5 cm, diameter: 22 cm
c. 1240

A shallow dish with a narrow flat rim and a convex centre, in which is a scene of Samson's struggle with the lion. The figures appear against a dark blue enamelled background; the foliated scrolls which surround them are not enamelled but filled in with engraved detail. Within the broad enamelled strip which runs round the convex sides of the dish are medallions separated by palmettes and scrolls. Winged and nimbed angels, decorated with engraving, appear in the medallions, the angels themselves are not enamelled; their backgrounds are enamelled in dark blue, decorated in pale blue, green, yellow, red and purple, as are the palmettes. An undulating line runs round the narrow flat enamelled rim.

Dishes of this type were produced in fairly large quantities in Limoges—their best period was between 1230 and 1270. They were generally produced in pairs for the washing of hands, both ceremonially at the Mass and at the tables of the nobility.

55 THE MARGARET ISLAND CROWN

Site: Margaret Island, church of the Dominican Convent, Budapest
Inv. No.: 1847. 43.a. KKO. Silver-gilt
Diameter: 17 cm, size of one section: 6.5 × 1.8 cm
Second half of the 13th century

The jewel was washed up in the great Pest flood of 1838 by which Margaret Island was inundated. It was found among the ruins of the Dominican Convent built for St. Margaret, a princess of the Árpád dynasty.

The head-band is made up of eight narrow plaques, joined by hinges; in the centre of each of these plaques, which have a plain undecorated surface, is a large flower, cut from plate silver. Their edges are serrated. Above each flower stands a fleur-de-lis, the tip of each of its petals set with a pearl held in a small decorative mount, the stone in the centre of each lily is a garnet. Large jewels in mounts of irregular shape are set at either side of each of the hinges; the pins which fasten the hinges are topped by three leaves cut from sheet silver and lightly engraved. The jewels themselves proved to be amethysts and garnets. Some of the pearls have crumbled into dust.

This relic is the most beautiful of the medieval royal funerary crowns. Because of its comparatively small size and narrow diameter it is considered to be a feminine crown. Judging from its design it was probably made in the seventies of the thirteenth century and was destined for the grave of one of the royal princesses buried on Margaret Island around that time. The crown is attributed to one of the skilful goldsmiths then working in the neighbouring royal workshop.

56 BELT BUCKLE AND BELT HARNESS

Site: Kígyóspuszta, Bács-Kiskun County
Inv. No.: 61.64.1–5. C. KKO. Gold and silver-gilt
Length: 10 cm
From the turn of the 13th–14th century

The rectangular gold plaque is attached to a silver-gilt oval buckle. The latter has two decorative knobs, designed to hold the pointed tongue of the buckle in place. The plaque holding the strap of the belt is made of double gold foil, the upper part decorated in niello with a battle scene of knights, dressed in authentic costumes and carrying authentic representations of arms, military standards, and shields with coats of arms of the second half of the thirteenth century. Soon after the completion of the belt this plaque was shortened a little so that the end of the scene was cut off.

Four round gold buttons belonging to the same belt are also decorated in niello, each of the obliquely cut frames surrounding the raised boss of the button bears one of the following inscriptions in Gothic majuscules:

S(ancte) BARTHOLOME ORA PRO M(e)
S(ancte) IACOBE ORA PRO ME
S(ancte) STEPHANE ORA PROME [sic]
S(ancta) MARGARETA ORA PRO ME

From the style of the lettering it seems probable that the four inscribed buttons were made at the time when the belt was repaired; they are examples of the slightly later style of the beginning of the fourteenth century.

The maker of the buckle and belt harness is not known but it may be assumed that he was a goldsmith practising in the Hungarian royal workshop.

57 BAPTISMAL FONT

Site: Liptótepla (Liptovská Teplá), Czechoslovakia
Inv. No.: 1914.132. KKO. Cast bronze
Height: 89 cm, diameter: 60.5 cm
Second half of the 14th century

The chalice-shaped font is cast in two separate pieces: the basin or cup and the bell-shaped foot joined to it by a flat boss. Its decoration is in the form of two horizontal stripes, the main motif being an inscription in capital letters, surrounding the vessel to form several circles. The inscription on the basin reads IN NOMINE PATRIS ET FILII + ET SPIRITUS SANCTI + AMEN +. Between and beneath the two lines, rows of undulating foliage with five-pointed leaves in the curls of the stem fill in the spaces. The same ornament, probably meant to represent a vine, is repeated on the lower rim of the foot and on the boss. Above the boss is a row of embossed octagons within which Greek crosses and rosettes alternate to form a pattern. The bell-shaped foot is covered by an inscription of five lines of capital letters.

The closest examples of baptismal fonts from the point of view of form and proportion are those in Svedlér (Şvedlár) and Szepesváralja (Spisšké Podhradie), produced by Konrád Gál, a metal founder *(campanista)* of Igló (Spišská Nová Ves). Similar features in form and decoration would seem to indicate that the Museum's baptisma font was also a product of the famous Igló workshop.

58 CIBORIUM

Site: Szepeskörtvélyes (Spišský Hrušov), Czechoslovakia
Inv. No.: 1916.31. KKO. Gilded copper
Height: 39 cm
Second half of the 14th century

On the foot, four rounded lobes alternate with four triangular projections. The slender stem is composed of undecorated hexagonal plaques; the flattened node is set with projecting square mounts holding garnets. The cup is made up of six square plaques on whose traced background are scenes of the Annunciation, Christ on the Mount of Olives, Christ before Pilate, the Betrayal of Christ, the Flogging and the Crucifixion. The piece is a typical example of the kind of pictorial representations that are found in the *Biblia pauperum :* devout but illiterate Christians learnt the Church's teachings from simply executed pictures; in this case the finely incised scenes are probably based on painted miniatures. The six sides of the pyramidal roof are also engraved with pictures executed in traced technique. They represent the apostles Peter and Paul together with four Doctors of the Church, each holding a large book. On the top of the ciborium is a more recent plain crucifix and the inscription INRI.

The ciborium was probably commissioned by the king. It was intended as a part of the furnishings of the Szepeskörtvélyes church built and consecrated round about this time.

59 MONSTRANCE

Site: Szendrő, Borsod-Abaúj-Zemplén County
Inv. No.: 1937. 4. KKO. Silver-gilt
Height: 65 cm, diameter of base: 14.3 cm
15th century

The drop-shaped compartments of its six-lobed base enclose incised representations of the most popular saints of the period: the Madonna and Child, St. Barbara, St. John the Baptist, St. Ladislas, St. John the Evangelist and St. Margaret of Scotland, a saint of Hungarian origin. The figures are shown wearing the fashionable dress of the fifteenth century, holding their attributes in their hands. Above the base, at the bottom of the shaft of the monstrance is a Gothic arcading made up of six recesses. Above this is a flat knop on which three enamelled rhomboids alternate with three blue enamel flowers.

The large and elaborate monstrance rests on a flanged rhomboidal supporting pillar. The lunette, for holding the Host, is enclosed behind an arched door which retains its original glass panes. The case, a copy of a Gothic church in miniature, is supported by buttresses on each side. The hexagonal tower is also architectural in inspiration; tracery tall narrow windows are surmounted by a spire with a projecting cornice with Gothic pinnacles in cast silver. On the point of the spire is a crucifix over which is the scroll with the inscription INRI.

The monstrance, a magnificent example in which the art of the goldsmith has found its most felicitous expression is, at the same time, the most typical specimen of the work of contemporary Hungarian goldsmiths.

The name of the master who actually made this piece is not known but in view of the excellence of its workmanship it is regarded as having been produced in the Hungarian royal workshop or in a studio influenced by it.

60 THE ERNUSTH CHALICE

Provenance unknown
Inv. No.: Cim.Sec. II.1.2. KKO. Silver-gilt
Height: 25.5 cm, diameter of mouth: 11 cm, diameter of base: 16.2 cm
c. 1480

The greater part of the decoration of the chalice consists of a thickly encrusted patterned surface made up, for the most part, of tiny elements imitating wood shavings. The chalice takes its name from the three coats of arms incised on its plain cup—first that of the family Ernusth of Csáktornya, bearing a crenellated rampart surmounted by two stars, secondly the Pálóczys' coat: a figure of a bearded man, holding a book and rising from a crown and thirdly the Rozgonyis' coat, a goose with wings displayed, also emerging from a crown.

Below the coats of arms the cup is held in an elaborate case, surmounted by an encircling wreath composed of fleur-de-lis set on a band of open-work Gothic ornament. The swelling case itself is covered with a close design of 'shavings', some of which resolve themselves into acanthus leaves. The curling foils of silver are interspersed with tiny garnets and pearls. Below the case, two cast and pierced rings form a part of the stem and are decorated with geometrical patterns. The knop of the chalice is ornamented with more 'shavings' while below it is a cast gothic arcading made up of six tall semicircular sections to resemble an ambulatory. From this emerges the six-lobed base, which broadens as it descends and is richly encrusted with 'shavings', garnets and pearls. It is separated from the rim of the base by a cast fillet with pierced tracery.

The rim bears the following engraved inscription: LEONARDUS CIANUS TRIDENT CATH. ECCL. VAC. CANON SACERD OB BENEFICIA GRATI ANIMI MON A XCI MDCCXCI REGIS OPUS FONUMQUE FUI POST SAECULA TANDEM ME TRIA GENS TENEAT CLARA MIGATIADUM.

From the collection published in the *Cimeliotheca*.

61 THURIBLE

Provenance unknown
Inv. No.: 1909.9.6. KKO. Bronze, cast
Height: 24.5 cm, greatest diameter: 10.2 cm
15th century

The thurible we see here consists of two parts: the pierced cover and the chalice-shaped lower part are held together by five chains which, higher up, are held together by links. A large oval ring on the top of the thurible served for suspension. Below this ring is a small roof, pierced with holes and below this again is a section composed of tall rectangular openings beneath which the cover broadens out to form an octagonal hemisphere. This is decorated with cut-out heart shapes, upright and reversed. The hemisphere is edged by a narrow incised ring below which the cover is continued in eight vertical planes, each decorated with three round holes and, below them, three rectangular holes. The chains, by which it was suspended, are threaded through five rings which project from the rim of the cover.

The lower half of the thurible has the character of a stocky Romanesque chalice. Its plain sides form an octagon where they meet the cover but are rounded into a hemisphere where they join the stem. This stands on an eight-lobed foot.

Thuribles formed the majority of the ecclesiastical objects produced by Hungarian bronzesmiths in the fourteenth and fifteenth centuries. This piece is outstanding both in the quality and the beauty of its workmanship.

62 STOVE TILE

Site: Besztercebánya (Banská Bystrica), Czechoslovakia
Inv. No.: 58/1894.2. KKO. Fired clay
Height: 24.5 cm, width: 22.2 cm
Second half of the 15th century

A square, unglazed stove tile, framed by a square border consisting of a wide curve forming a recess, within which is a further recessed band between two narrow ridges. The figure of St. John the Evangelist modelled in relief appears within this frame, his halo and drapery overlapping its inner elements. His torso, turned left, is partly covered by a cloak; his face is framed between falling corkscrew curls. Rising behind his head, a halo is decorated with a ring of fine beading. The right hand is lifted to hold his cloak against his chest, the left holds an angular chalice with a ribbed foot. From the cup emerges a serpent.

This subject, especially the hair and the garments of the saint, are closely related to contemporary medieval wood-carvings.

63 GOBLET OF KING MATTHIAS

Provenance unknown
Inv. No.: 1929.9. KKO. Glass with a silver-gilt foot
Height: 43 cm, diameter of mouth: 27.5 cm, diameter of base: 23 cm
Second half of the 15th century

Originally the whole goblet was made of glass, a typical product of the Venetian glass industry of the end of the fifteenth century. The small bubbles in the glass are probably due to its very large size. The upper, funnel-shaped part is plain; it is joined by a wide knob of striped glass to the silver-gilt foot, which curves outwards and was attached at a later period to the goblet.

There had, at one time, been some small turquoises on the upper part of the foot but only a few remain. The foot, as it spreads out, bears the engraved inscription: VINA BIBANT HOMINES ANIMALIA COETERA FONTES (Man should drink wine, other animals water).

Also engraved on the foot is a circular inscription in Hungarian, beginning with the words "This is King Matthias's goblet, an old gift bought from Venetians...", tells the story of the fifteenth-century goblet which passed from Matthias Corvinus, through King Louis to Ferenc Battyani. The greater part of the inscription sings the praises of the heroic deeds of this prominent member of the Battyani family (1497–1566). It may therefore be assumed that it was he who had the foot made.

64 CAPITAL WITH INSCRIBED SCROLLS

Site: Buda Castle Hill, surroundings of Buda Town Hall (2, Szentháromság Street)
Inv. No.: 1875/282 and 61.71.C. KKO. Red marble
Dimensions: 54×57×53 cm, upper diameter: 60 cm, lower diameter: 45 cm
Last third of the 15th century

The surface was cracked by fire and the upper corners are broken. The top has been hollowed out and it may have been used as a second baptismal font at the Matthias Church, near the site of which the capital was found.

Below the covering slab which forms a square with concave sides, an egg-and-dart border encircles the capital. At the corners this border is partly concealed by inscribed scrolls, ending in volutes. The capital, composed of four square planes rising from a circular base, is embellished with an arrangement of vertical inscribed scrolls, which curve away from each other in opposite directions. The ends of the scrolls are only partially unrolled, from the pair of ends nearest the base of the capital grows a small floral ornament; large acanthus leaves, whose tips curl outwards, support the scrolls. The scrolls bear the inscription: MATHIAS PRINC (EPS I) NVICTVS INGEN(II V)OLVPTATI OPVS HOC CONDIDIT GENEROSVM (King Matthias, the invincible, raised this noble creation to the delight of the spirit).

This architectural capital, which is not overburdened with superfluous ornament, fits well into the architectural style current in Buda during the Renaissance.

65 MEDIEVAL TOOLS

14th–16th centuries

ANVIL

Site: Gerjen, Fehérároki dűlő, Tolna County
Inv. No.: 69.52.C. KKO. Forged iron
Length: 21.5 cm, upper surface: 19 × 9 cm, under surface: 13 × 6.7 cm

A rectangular block, narrowing towards the base; gently curving sides. The upper surface is slightly convex.

PLOUGHSHARE AND COULTER

Site: Máriabesnyő, Pest County
Inv. No.: 60.4.1–2. C. KKO. Forged iron
Ploughshare, length: 31 cm, width: 17.5 cm
Coulter, length: 47.5 cm, width of blade: 7.8 cm

The ploughshare is fairly long and triangular in shape; its slightly asymmetrical blade is convex at the back. The two wings of its short broad socket curve slightly down.

The handle of the coulter is straight and its short, slightly broadening blade curved; its point is rounded.

AXE

Site: Máriabesnyő, Pest County
Inv. No.: 60.4.3. C. KKO. Forged iron
Length: 22.3 cm, width of blade: 12.8 cm, length of socket: 11 cm

The socket is rectangular in cross-section. Both sides are flush with the neck and the two sides of the blade. The blade is gently curved, its outside edge is at right angles to the socket; its inner edge is curved. The socket is long and narrow.

CARPENTER'S HATCHET

Site: Zsámbék, Pest County
Inv. No.: HN. 14/1912.4. KKO. Forged iron
Length: 19 cm, width of blade: 11.5 cm, length of socket: 8 cm

The left-hand blade is flush with the long rectangular wall of the socket; the right is a little bent at the point where the socket joins the neck. The upper edge is at right angles to the socket, the lower edge follows a broken line. The tool has a short narrow neck and a comparatively broad blade. A square head with a flattened end is forged on to the rear of the socket. Between the blade and the neck there is a trilobate hole which serves as a nail-claw. On the right side is stamped the master's mark—three convex points in a stylized leaf pattern; on the inner corner is an incised half-moon and a stamped star-shaped mark, perhaps to denote its owner.

156

66 BOOKCASE

Site: St. Giles' Church, Bártfa (Bardejov), Czechoslovakia
Inv. No.: 6/1915; 63.1.C. KKO. Lime and larch wood carved and painted
Height: 238 cm, width: 53 cm, length: 428 cm
c. 1487

Each of the six compartments, which are of equal size, is closed by a door. Along its entire length the top of the bookcase is embattled above a broad band of *relief en creux* in a regularly repeating pattern of four-petalled, quadrifoliate stylized flowers joined by small-petalled round roses. Both the border and the battlements, which lend a lightness to the whole design, are polychrome. The front of the bookcase is flat and divided by uprights decorated by a polychrome design of foliage coiled round a vertical branch. The surface of the doors themselves is enlivened by the fittings which consist of iron lockplates painted brown and ornamented with lilies, tin-plated iron hinges with a pierced pattern and cast bronze handles. The inside is divided by shelves and partitions.

The historic and cultural importance of the bookcase is greatly enhanced by the fact that it contains 75 books of its original stock which have survived from the fifteenth and sixteenth centuries. The incunabula and some of the manuscript codices, still in their original bindings, include not only basic ecclesiastical works but also several books on history, law, astronomy and mathematics. Originally a church library, the books passed, during the period of the Reformation, into municipal ownership, becoming consequently accessible to the public. It could be regarded thus as the first public library of medieval Hungary.

67 TURKISH LEATHER CLOAK

Inv. No.: 69.80.C. KKO. Leather with coloured leather appliqué
Length measured at the edge of the side panel: 115 cm, at the back: 125 cm
First half of the 16th century

Bought by the Hungarian National Museum in 1969 from Mária Esterházy, widow of János Almásy.

The cloak is made up of several panels which widen towards the hem. They are sewn together as far down as the waist; from the waist down they are left open. The front consists of two panels which are folded back to their full width and are trimmed with a delicate pattern of appliqué. The pattern which runs down the borders consists of eight shorter and eight longer motifs. The corners of the front panels are filled with delicately cut patterns of large flowers, each grouped round a central flower. The flowers on the collar are embroidered in gold thread. The sleeves are short. The back of the cloak is cut to form an ogee arch in which is a stylized lily outlined in green cord.

In view of the fact that it is cut open to the waist, it is probable that the robe was worn as a riding-coat.

68 ECCLESIASTICAL CHOIR STALLS

Site: Nyírbátor, Szabolcs-Szatmár County. From the chancel of St. George's Church
Inv. No.: 67/1933 a.c. KKO. Oak with carving in low and high relief and marquetry
Height: 400 cm, length: 1,025+200 cm
1511

In the back row there are twelve seats above the access passage and two below it; in front of the bookrest is a row of eleven seats, again divided by the opening. All the seats are divided from each other by thick curving armrests. The tall back of the stalls consists of panels divided by engaged pilasters surmounted by a frieze above which is a canopy composed of rounded arches, one to each seat. Above the arches runs a richly ornamented cornice. The decoration on the seats in the front row, below the bookrest, corresponds to that on the back, the panels below the seats are carved in low relief with imaginatively assembled motifs familiar in Renaissance architecture. They include egg-and-dart borders, beading, dolphins, arabesque of branches carrying flowers and thickly clustering leaves, bunches of fruit, candelabra, plaits of cording, cherubs' heads, lion-masks and many more, as well as the dragon-toothed coat of arms of the Báthori family. The inlaid panels of the back are especially interesting. Besides those represented in the Báthori coat of arms, there are symbolic human and animal images and plants, framed by a variety of geometrical patterns. The panels representing a half-open cupboard door revealing books, vessels, goldsmiths' work and pomegranates on shelves inside, are outstanding examples of marquetry. The name of the master-craftsman; F. MA-RONE, is legible on the spine of one of the books. Another panel bears the names and ranks of the three Báthori brothers: György, István and András, who commissioned Marone to undertake the work, and the date of its creation: 1511. The counterpart to these stalls, which is incomplete and without a canopy is, for the present, deposited in the Báthori Museum in Nyírbátor.

This masterpiece, produced by one of the foremost members of a famous Florentine Renaissance workshop of joiners and carvers, which also carried out orders for the Hungarian court, represents the only piece of Renaissance furniture to survive in Hungary.

69 EARTHENWARE JUG

Site: Szécsény, Nógrád County
Inv. No. 64.3.C. KKO. Yellowish-white clay with incised decoration
Height: 29 cm
First half of the 16th century

A tall, slender jug, the upper half glazed. It rises from the base to a swelling belly and continues to a high shoulder from which rises the neck which supports a moderately wide rim, with a lip. Surrounding the base is an impressed pattern produced by means of a cog-wheel, above and parallel with it are two closely-set incised lines. The rim is equally decorated with a cog-wheel pattern above which are three incised lines. A strap-like handle springs from below the rim to join the belly of the jug just above its widest point. The handle is ornamented with a row of very small circles. The glazed area, from the belly to the rim, is divided into three horizontal fields by incised lines, each field is differently patterned. The outside of the upper part of the jug, the inside of the mouth and the handle are covered by a brownish-yellow glaze: the glazing of the incised decoration and of the narrow strip on the outside below the rim is pale green.

After the death of King Matthias Corvinus the masters who worked in the royal workshops were dispersed and continued to pursue their craft in various parts of the country. The Szécsényi jug can be traced back to the traditions of their time.

70 GUILD BADGE

Place of origin: Brassó (Brașov), Rumania
Inv. No.: 1887.67. KKO. Cast silver with engraved repoussé
Height: 16 cm
1556

Made of thick silver plate in the form of a shield cut at the two sides into semicircular curves. At the top there are two rings by means of which it could be hung up; below them are two small globules ornamented with leaves. The upper edge of the plaque takes the form of an undulating curve below which is a straight band decorated with incised leaves in the centre of which is a moustached mask. A similar band of incised leaves runs across the bottom of the plaque and terminates in a point. The whole plaque is framed by a silver rim soldered on to the base. Between the two horizontal bands of incised leaves is a pictorial scene representing a goldsmith's shop modelled in high relief. The goldsmith, wearing the dress of his time, is shown in the act of hammering a goblet on an anvil. To his left is a small table on which stands a jar, a pot with a cover and a moulding iron. Under the table is a second anvil. Behind the goldsmith and to his right is another table on which are bowls, moulding irons and wire-drawing tools. Under this table are a bucket and another vessel, probably used for casting. Above the table a pair of bellows hangs on the wall.

Beneath this scene, in the lower border of leaves, an owl appears together with the initials IE. On the back of the shield is an engraved scene which represents a goldsmith's shop—based on a sixteenth century engraving. It shows the master and his journeyman, another man leaning on his elbow in a window, two quarrelling youngsters, and includes an anvil and goldsmiths' tools.

Apart from its high artistic merit, the interest of this guild sign lies in the fact that no other goldsmith's work of the kind has survived. It should be possible to trace the name of the master craftsman who made it through the initials IE but so far he has not been identified among the goldsmiths of Brassó.

71 RENAISSANCE JEWELLERY
17th century

ROSETTE
Inv. No.: Orn. Jank. 122. KKO. Gold and black enamel
Diameter: 6 cm

The six petal-like loops of the rosette are enamelled with a design of flowers; in the centre are six oval daisies, each set with a diamond at its centre and enamelled in red, blue and green. Within this circle of daisies is a square-cut diamond, surrounded by six small black petals. The threads between the loops of the rosette are enamelled in blue, white and black.

NECKLACE
Inv. No.: Orn. Jank. 204. KKO. Gold
Length: 32.2 cm

The necklace consists of 27 links enamelled in black and white; rosettes set with emeralds alternate with narrow white enamel leaves—the rosettes and the leaves are separated by pearls. The black and white enamelled pendant which hangs in the middle is composed of enamelled leaves and is set with two pearls.

BROOCH
Inv. No.: 60.177.C. KKO. Gold, Transylvanian enamel, set with almandines
Height: 11 cm, width: 7 cm

A bouquet of six-petalled flowers. The centre of the large flower at the top is an almandine surrounded by a wreath of black and white enamelled leaves; the petals spring from groups of almandines. In the centre of each of the three small flowers is a jewel. The four leaves are composed of translucent enamel; where the stems of the flowers meet is an almandine.

AIGRETTE
Inv. No.: Pig. Jank. 242. KKO. Gold and coloured enamel
Height: 15.8 cm

The upper part is enamelled in blue and white to represent four plumes, the smallest of them leans towards the right. Each plume has a row of rubies as its central rib and, where the fronds of the feathers meet, are pearls. The lower part of the aigrette is a large rosette also set with pearls, rubies and, suspended on tiny rings, four pearl drops. The stem of the aigrette is of champlevé enamel and the back of the jewel is also of coloured enamel. All these pieces of jewellery are typical of the jewels worn by members of the Transylvanian aristocracy. They are the work of Hungarian goldsmiths.

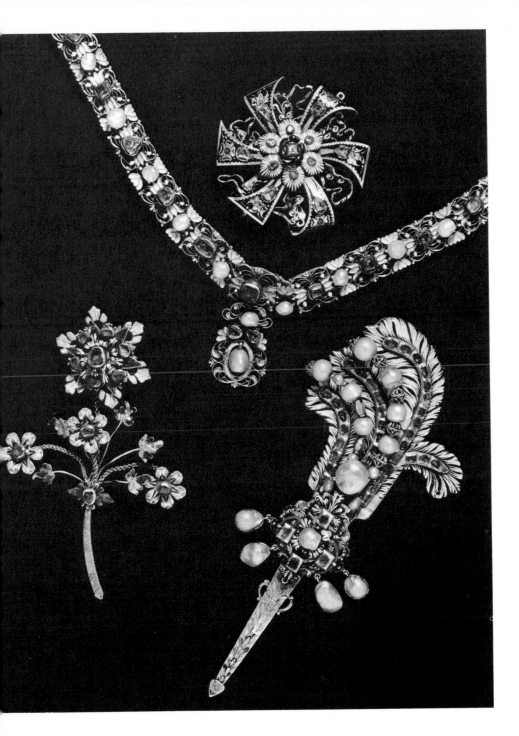

72 GOBLET WITH COVER

Provenance unknown
Inv. No.: 53.46 KKO. Silver-gilt, enamelled
Height: 26 cm, diameter of foot: 7.6 cm, diameter of mouth: 7 cm
17th century

An ornamental network of leaves and flowers, executed in so-called 'Transylvanian' enamelling, covers practically the whole of the goblet and its cover.

On the top of the lid is a sculptured bouquet whose spreading flowers are worked in coloured enamel; the stigmas are of pearls. The shallow dome-shaped upper part of the cover is ornamented with a double garland in blue, yellow, violet, brown and black enamel, on a white base. The cup follows the shape of contemporary chalices, though its form is slightly more slender. Its decoration consists of two horizontal bands of large tulips and marguerites emerging between curling leaves. This cup is supported on volutes which rest on the upper part of the stem, shaped like an inverted pear and enamelled; below that again is an enamelled garland which rests on an undecorated funnel-shaped part of the stem, leading to the foot of the goblet, which is also decorated with an enamel garland. Round the edge of both the foot and the cover the so far unidentified initials HH. The goldsmith who made this goblet must have been one of the outstanding masters among the members of the Transylvanian goldsmith's guild.

73 TURKISH SILVER CUP

Provenance unknown
Inv. No. 55.446. C. KKO. Beaten silver
Height: 3.3 cm, diameter: 12.2 cm

In the centre of the bowl is a shallow depression in which lies a circle occupied by a large engraved wading bird, seen in profile, stepping out on long legs among flowers and leaves; surrounding this circle is a band of interlaced strapwork, from which spring ten engraved stripes, ornamented with engraved flowers and leaves, curving upwards to meet the rim of the bowl round which is a border of semicircles. Beneath the rim can be seen the master's mark: *amel-i-Mustafa* (made by Mustafa).

The size of this elaborately pounced and chased bowl makes it clear that it served as a drinking cup. In the centuries that followed, eastern peoples attributed magic properties to vessels such as this, believing that they protected them from disease and even from the evil eye.

74 THE BRÓZER CHALICE

Place of origin: Kolozsvár (Cluj-Napoca), Rumania
Inv. No.: 1926.90. Gold with cloisonné and colour enamel
Height: 26 cm, diameter of mouth: 10.4 cm, diameter of bottom: 11 cm
1640

A chalice with attached embossed plaques and pierced decoration in cloisonné and coloured enamel. The lid is missing. On the rim two lines of engraved inscription consisting of quotations from the Bible read: POCULUM BENEDICTIONIS CIU BENEDICIMUS NONNE COMMUNIO SANGVINIS CHRISTI EST I. COR. X. VER. 16.
BIBITE EX HOC OMNES MATTH. 26. VER. 27.
HOC POCULUM EST NOVUM ILLUD PACTUM PER MEUM SANGVINEM SANCT. PAUL. I. CORINTUS II. vers. 25.

On the cup itself are eighteen oval-shaped plaques depicting the Passion of Christ from the Last Supper to the Entombment. Between the attached plaques the spaces are enriched with a formal design which includes garlands of foliage in exquisitely coloured enamel-work which produces an effect of great magnificence. On the knop and on the rings on the stem, the enamel, mainly blue in colour, was poured into an engraved gold plate. On the raised foot of the chalice there are foliated and floral designs attached with tiny rivets which are examples of the seventeenth century goldsmiths' favourite technique, known as Transylvanian enamelling.

Inside the chalice, imposed on the arms of Transylvania, in coloured enamel, are the arms of the Rákóczi family and an inscription indicates that the chalice was commissioned by György Rákóczi I, Prince of Transylvania, for the Calvinist Church at Kolozsvár (Cluj-Napoca). According to the inscription inside the stem, which reads *"Colosvárat Brózer István czinálta Anno 1640"*. (It was made by István Brózer at Kolozsvár in the year 1640.)

75 THE RÁKÓCZI TANKARD

Provenance unknown
Inv. No.: 1939.27. KKO. Silver-gilt and cut glass
Height: 23 cm, diameter of mouth: 10.5 cm, diameter of foot: 12.5 cm
17th century

The cover is domed in the centre, the dome supported on a rounded, bulging ring which in turn rests on the flat plate which serves as the actual lid. Rising from the central dome s an enamelled flower with open petals, holding in its centre a small glass knob. The twelve-sided body of the tankard is of cut crystal glass; down the edge of every second side a silver-gilt band descends from a plain rim at the top to a decorative ring at the bottom, thus forming an open outer silver case in which the glass tankard is held. Among the subjects which are cut in the polished glass sides of the tankard is one which depicts a castle with six towers; two panels are patterned with daisies; in three others a floral design alternates with hearts and in another there is a pair of pigeons perched on a branch. The base of the glass tankard fits into the enamelled frame and is held by a band of semicircles curving upwards, below which is a convex border of alternating enamelled and repoussé leaves, typical of the beautiful Transylvanian coloured enamel work. A narrow enamelled scroll runs down the S-shaped handle.

Inside the cover an embossed plate indicates that the tankard was made for Prince Rákóczi. The inscription reads as follows: FRANCISCUS DEI GRA(TIA) PRINC (EPS) RAKOCZI COM(ES) DE SAAR(OS) DUX MUNK(ACIENSIS) ET MAKOV (ICENSIS) DOM(INUS) PER(PETUUS) DE SAROSPATOK REG(ECZ) EC(SED) SOM(LYO).

Tradition has it that Ferenc Rákóczi II made a present of the tankard to a member of the Luzsénszky family.

76 BÁLINT FRANK'S TANKARD AND COVER

Place of origin: Nagyszeben (Sibiu), Rumania
Inv. No.: 1874.261.2. KKO. Silver-gilt
Height: 29.5 cm, diameter of mouth: 12.7 cm, diameter of foot: 15.3 cm
1697

The tankard is constructed from two plates of silver. On the centre of the cover is a free-standing sculptured figure of a knight on a rearing horse; round him, on the cover itself, three children lie on branches of roses.

The tankard is embossed in high relief with three scenes: (1) the sacrifice of Marcus Curtius; (2) Croesus sent to the stake by Cyrus but saved from death; (3) the story of Perillus who perished inside the metal bull he had invented. Above and below these scenes, and round the base of the tankard are engraved inscriptions referring to the scenes portrayed.

Round the base is an interesting text in German which reads:
Hermannstad ist durch die Kunst
dieses Meisters Augspurg worden.
Lebe lang Sebastian Hann
In Werther Menschen Orden.
praising the maker's merits.

On the inside of the cover the titles of Hann's employer, VALENTINUS FRANCK de FRANKENSTEIN, and the name of the person to whom he presented it: NEPOTI SUO VALENTINO are inscribed.

Sebastian Hann, the Nagyszeben master, produced several large tankards similar to this one, decorated with scenes in relief, which have given him the reputation of being one of the outstanding goldsmiths of his period.

178

Date of foundation :	1952
Collections :	Historical costumes and textiles
	Goldsmiths' work
	Weapons
	Furniture
	Ceramics, porcelain and glass
	Musical instruments
	Clocks and instruments
	Seals
	History of smoking
	Pewter
	Toys
	History of industry
	Household utensils
	Historical records and documents of the modern period
Number of items :	41,831

MODERN HISTORY DEPARTMENT

The collections preserved in the Modern Department stretch back to the foundation of the Museum itself and have been added to ever since. The basic collections from the old Historical Repository now form a valuable part of the material housed in the Modern Department.

The Department is charged with the collection and preservation of relics of the cultural development of Hungarian society, objects associated with outstanding figures, progressive personalities of the past and other material of historic interest. Its field of interest extends to relics and remains neglected by the Museum in earlier days, such as objects connected with the activities of manual workers, peasants, etc. Since 1967, its collecting activities in the field of contemporary history have been covered by official regulations. This has turned the Department into the custodian of Modern and Contemporary History.

During the past twenty-five years some of the collections—textiles, weapons, musical instruments and goldsmiths' work for example—have become, at a national level, unique in their particular categories. A considerable number of objects, as, for instance, the pianos of Beethoven and Liszt, the barytone owned by Haydn, the attire of Louis II and Queen Maria of Hungary, dress, coif and virginal of Catherine of Brandenburg, Apafi's backgammon-board, the armour of Louis II of Hungary, the sabre of Ferdinand of Tyrol, are of European significance in the fields of history and social history.

The restorers employed by the Department, whose activity cover the conservation of furniture, textile and, more recently—for the first time in Hungary—that of musical instruments, accomplish the task of restoring to their original beauty many pieces of outstanding value with remarkable success.

The recording and documentation carried out by the Department has been no less important.

Members of the Department have also been responsible for organizing two permanent exhibitions opened in 1951 and 1967, "Hungary's History from the Magyar Conquest to 1849", and have also played a part in the organization of large temporary exhibitions, both in Hungary and abroad—Tekirdag, Turin, Shumen and other places.

Imre Bánkúti

77 THRONE-CARPET

Inv. No.: 1960.190. Gold brocade
Size: 254×162 cm
1470's

After the death of the King Matthias Corvinus the carpet came into the possession of Archbishop Tamás Bakócz. It was later acquired by the Erdődy family who presented It to the Hungarian National Museum.

The carpet, which is brocaded in gold with a design outlined in green velvet, is woven of yellow and green silk, the entire surface brocaded in gold, some areas of which are composed of uncut loops of gold thread.

The border is formed by a pattern of wings, cornucopias and ears of wheat. The central design, round which the formal pattern is composed, consists of the quartered arms of King Matthias Corvinus, which include, beyond the arms of Hungary, those of Dalmatia and Bohemia: the escutcheon displays the family arms of the Hunyadis: the raven.

The arms are enclosed in a wreath of oak-leaves, pears and pomegranates, from either side of the upper part of which two cornucopias emerge from knots of ribbon; they hold pears and pomegranates from which grow flowering briar-rose branches.

In the middle of the lower part a richly articulated ornamental vessel standing on a marble pedestal is flanked by two eagles taking wing. The tasselled ribbon of the wreath undulates above their heads.

This carpet was woven to a design by Antonio Pollaiuolo and produced in the workshop of Francesco Malocchi, in Florence. It is an outstanding specimen of Italian Renaissance woven brocade.

King Matthias owned several of these throne-cloths of which only this one has survived in its entirety. A second was cut up to make a chasuble and two fragments of a third are in the collection of the Hungarian National Museum.

78 CHASUBLE

Inv. No.: 1908.70. Velvet, embroidered
Back length: 140 cm, width 76 cm; front length: 98 cm, width 62 cm
Between 1480 and 1500

The chasuble was bought by the Museum from the church of Sztropkó (Stropkov).
The cross on the back is embroidered in the finest needlework on a plain red velvet
ground. Christ enthroned in Judgement is seated against a gold background under a
trefoil arch. Below is Golgotha. On one side of the short limb of the cross the Virgin
kneels, behind her the blessed souls; on the other side St. John the Baptist with the
damned. The long limb of the cross is lengthened at the base where there appears a
mutilated scene of the Annunciation, which probably at one time decorated the front
of the chasuble. The drawing of the figures reveals strong Flemish influence.

79 LADY'S GOWN AND CHEMISE

Inv. No.: 1928.36 and 38. The dress, silk damask; the chemise, linen, embroidered
Length to waist in front: 30 cm, at the back: 36 cm, skirt-length, front: 107 cm, back: 124 cm, sleeve-length: 71 cm
1522

The wedding-dress of Queen Maria, wife of Louis II, 1522. Bought by the Hungarian National Museum in 1928 from the treasury of the votive church of Maria-Zell.

The dress is of green silk damask with a Renaissance design of large palmettes within which are pomegranates surrounded by small marguerite flowers. This type of silk damask was woven in Florence in the second half of the fifteenth century. The bodice of the dress fits closely and is open in front in a very wide V-shape; this cut was designed to show off to advantage the short-waisted tall slender figure, fashionable at the time. At the back the neck is cut to a low oval. The sleeves are long and straight with funnel-shaped cuffs which fall over the hands; a narrow braid of gold edges the neckline and the cuffs. The long trained circular skirt is joined to the bodice by a seam at the waist. The style of the dress reflects to some extent what can loosely be regarded as the Renaissance fashion of the time.

The chemise, which reaches to the ankles, is of very fine linen, gathered closely into an approximately square neckline and with very full sleeves which also reach the neckline. A band of ornamental embroidery runs across the front of the chemise. Both its cut and decoration are typical of late fifteenth century Italian chemises.

80 MAN'S GOWN AND CHEMISE

Inv. No.: 1928.35 and 37. The gown, woven brocade; the shirt, embroidered linen
Length of gown, front: 124 cm, back: 161 cm; sleeve: 113 cm; length of chemise: 139 cm
1522

King Louis II of Hungary wore these garments on the occasion of his wedding in 1522. Until 1928 it was kept in the treasury of the votive church of Maria-Zell, at which date it was purchased by the Hungarian National Museum.

The gown is of yellow and violet silk, double brocade and drawn gold. The fine outlines of the design are violet; its conspicuous elements are interwoven with gold; the background of the design is of plain gold. The reverse of the cloth is white silk damask interwoven with drawn silver, in a design composed of double foliated scrolls woven in a fine outline. The scrolls are connected by rows of petals and acanthus leaves, and in their centres are rosettes surrounded by wild roses, between which are roses blossoming among spirals of foliage. This type of design, in the Renaissance style, appears fairly frequently in brocades woven in Florence in the second half of the fifteenth century.

In front the gown reaches the calves; its pleated back slightly trails on the ground. The small turned-down collar shows the brocade on its reverse side. The sleeves, slit open up to the shoulder, hang to the level of the hem of the gown in front. Gowns of this cut were fashionable all over Europe during the fifteenth and the first third of the sixteenth century.

The ankle-length chemise which is a part of the costume is of fine cambric. At the wrist its long puffed sleeves are edged with a frill ornamented with faggot-stitching and gold embroidery. A stylized foliated and floral design in flat gold embroidery decorates the high up-standing collar, and the front on either side of the opening, as well as forming a band round the wrists above the frill.

81 CHASUBLE

Inv. No.: 1915. 64. Brocade, embroidered
Back length: 115 cm, width: 78 cm: front length: 109 cm, width: 71 cm
Beginning of the 16th century

The chasuble came to the Museum from the Kőszeg church. In Hungarian needlework, following a general use of couching, besides satin stitch, raised work became widely used in the decoration of chasubles in the sixteenth century. The chasuble itself is made of red and gold brocade of Italian manufacture; the woven design includes confronted cornucopias filled with fruit. On the back of the chasuble, embroidered with stump-work, is the Virgin and Child in glory, surrounded by a mandorla composed of rays; the Virgin stands on the crescent moon and is crowned by angels. On either side, in a quatrefoil, are half-length figures of the apostles St. John and St. Andrew and in the centre above, St. Anne with the young Virgin and the Child Jesus. Below the corbel supporting the Virgin and Child is a full-length figure of St. James. On the front of the chasuble the same three male saints are embroidered in relief. This vestment, which reveals strong German influence, is the finest surviving example of a Hungarian chasuble embroidered with raised work.

82 CHASUBLE

Inv. No.: 1935.42. Silk, embroidered
Length: 128 cm, width: 84 cm
1670

Cherry-red satin embroidered in gold and silver thread. The back of the chasuble is divided vertically into three bands, separated by a very narrow line of foliage and tiny flowers; the whole is surrounded by a border of arches each enclosing either a trefoil or a minute tulip. The central band of the chasuble is embroidered with a central stem from which spring, symmetrically on either side, tulips, columbines, lilies of the valley, carnations and leaves. The bands at the two sides contain embroidered scrolls filled with pomegranates and carnations. At the foot of the central band are the arms of the Károlyi and Sennyey families; on the front the date 1670 is embroidered. The geometrical pattern of the embroidery is carried out mainly in couching. It is the work of a Hungarian craftsman well acquainted with Renaissance decoration.

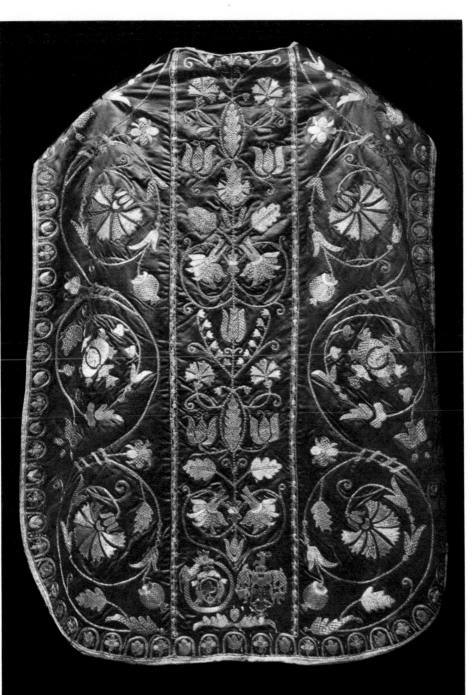

83 LADY'S GALA DRESS

Inv. No.: 1954.664. Velvet, embroidered
Length of skirt: 108 cm, length of bodice, front: 29 cm, back: 32 cm, waist: 43 cm
17th century

The dress was made for the second consort of Gábor Bethlen, Prince of Transylvania, round about 1626. Bethlen married Catherine of Brandenburg in 1626 and it was for this occasion that he had a dress of Hungarian style and cut made for her in Transylvania. The coif, which belongs to the costume, is worked with strings of real pearls in a pattern of tulips and rosettes, studded with enamelled spangles and table-emeralds.

The dress is made of plum-coloured cut and uncut velvet, woven in a design of alternating bushes whose branches are laden with tulips, acanthus leaves and pomegranates. Velvets woven in Italy at this period show a marked similarity in design to Hungarian domestic embroideries of the kind used for decorating table-cloths, altar-cloths and saddle-cloths.

The skirt, composed of straight panels, is held into the waist in large unpressed pleats. The waistline of the bodice is straight, the neck cut square. The narrow fronts of the bodice, with their wide lacing, are stiffened with bands of steel and horn and edged with embroidery. The skirt is ornamented with eight horizontal bands of embroidery in gold and silver thread in a design which is a larger version of that which trims the bodice; rosettes and carnations stand beneath arches which are separated by small tulips, based on a narrow border of scrolls and minute tulips. This decoration is an outstanding example of the type of Hungarian needlework made by the nobility and known as "domestic embroidery", distinguishing it from peasant work. It flourished in the sixteenth and seventeenth centuries and shows the influence of Italian Renaissance design. A chemise of cambric or gossamer, drawn into full gathers at the low neckline, and an apron of the same material trimmed with lace, were worn with the dress.

The wide apron closely gathered into folds, reached the hem of the skirt, the metal embroidery of which, as it glistened through the fine linen, increased the beauty of the whole costume which, in spite of its rich decoration, has a certain noble modesty.

84 TABLE-CLOTH (Detail)

Inv. No.: 1932.121. Silk velvet and gold embroidery
Size: 200 × 182 cm
Second quarter of the 17th century

This green and red velvet table-cloth with couched embroidery in gold and silver was made for Zsuzsanna Lorántffy, wife of György Rákóczi I, Prince of Transylvania.

The centre of the cloth, which is green, is almost completely covered with floral motifs; in the corners bouquets of flowers, bordered by small leaves, are striking examples of a Renaissance interpretation of a Persian design. The three-branched flower bouquet within the wreath of leaves is reminiscent of Italian design but here, too, Persian art has exerted an influence. In the middle of the cloth the arms of Transylvania and, *sur-le-tout*, the arms of the Lorántffy family.

In the red velvet border, two different types of design which combine the idiom of east and west, as well as the small floral motifs which fill in the spaces in the central area of the cloth, are characteristic of the type of embroidery made by the nobility and known in Hungary as "domestic embroidery". The table-cloth is the work of a professional master-embroiderer.

85 LADY'S DRESS

Inv. No.: 1961.3044. Silk, embroidered
Length of skirt: 138 cm, length of bodice: 28 cm
18th century

This dress was made for a member of the Kazinczy family. Its brown skirt, which has a short train, is cut from seven widths of silk (width: 60 cm). The delicately coloured embroidery, in which tall sprays of flowers and foliage are linked by floral scrolls, covers two-thirds of the skirt. The close-fitting bodice, laced up in the front, is decorated with narrow bands of embroidered flowers and leaves. All the embroidery, which includes very naturalistic representations of various kinds of flowers, is carried out in coloured silks.

86 LADY'S GALA DRESS

Inv. No.: 1935.109. Silk brocade
Length of the skirt: 106 cm
Middle of the 18th century

A dress worn by a member of the Majthényi family in about 1750.

The skirt, made up of straight lengths of silk gathered at the waist, is a sky-blue and silver Lyons brocade with an interwoven design of large flowers and leaves in violet, pink, yellow and green. The taffeta bodice, stiffened by closely set whaleboning, curves downwards at the waistline in front. The neckline is round, the front has a wide lacing over an attached stomacher and is trimmed with gold braid, 3 cm wide. The lace is held by fifteen silver hooks down each side. The dress was worn over a white cambric chemise with elbow-length sleeves caught into double puffs; round its neck and falling from the elbow are lace frills. The apron, gathered into close folds, has a deep lace edging.

The cut of Hungarian women's dress in the eighteenth century differed little from that worn in the seventeenth century, the main difference was merely that the bodice became longer in front so that it overlapped the skirt. The sleeves of the chemise were shorter and tied round to form two puffs. The fabric of which eighteenth-century gala dresses were made was usually French brocade with an interwoven floral pattern, which meant that they were no longer decorated with embroidery; bodices, however, were richly ornamented with rows of gold braid or, alternatively, with bobbin lace of gold or silver thread.

87 CHILD'S SUIT AND HIGH CAP

Inv. No.: 1954.667.1–4. Silk with a woven pattern
Length of knee-breeches: 46 cm, length of dolman: 43 cm, length of *mente:* 63.5 cm, height of cap: 32 cm
Around 1745

According to tradition the suit shown here belonged to the Emperor Joseph II as a child.

The suit is made of pale blue corded silk with a small widely-spaced pattern of flowers. The style follows the Hungarian fashion; the dolman is tight-fitting with long tight sleeves and a narrow stand-up collar, the right front is cut to a slant, in the Hungarian "shako" shape, and the triangle thus formed has a large motif in the corner of silver bobbin lace of the same fan-design as the lace which borders the hem, collar and front of the dolman, edged with a narrow silver braid. The fronts are fastened with wide frogging in silver; the buttons and loops are also silver. The cuffs are covered with cloth of silver.

The decoration of the ankle-length *mente* (sleeved overcoat) is similar to that of the dolman. The trousers are tight knee-breeches.

The cap, with a broad turned-up brim, has a long point which falls over the cap to one side and ends in a tassel.

88 GENTLEMAN'S GALA SUIT

Inv. No.: 1934.327. 1–2. Silk, embroidered
Length of dolman: 77 cm, length of *mente :* 94 cm
Third quarter of the 18th century

Worn by Sámuel Teleki, Chancellor of Transylvania.
Made of green corded silk, embroidered in yellow, green and white silk and gold thread. The front of the closely-fitting dolman is cut diagonally (shako shaped); it has a standing collar and at the end of the tight sleeves the cuffs are turned back. The dolman is fastened down the front with fourteen loops with braided buttons. Parallel with the fastening a narrow border of minute flowers runs up either side of the front. The cut and ornamentation of the *mente* (a type of sleeved overcoat) are similar to those of the dolman. Its collar, cuffs and hem are trimmed with fur.

The low ankle-boots (Inv. No.: 1926.46.1–2) are of black leather laced up the inner sides and decorated with embroidery in gold and silver.

Hungarian gala suits of the third quarter of the eighteenth century show the influence of the French fashion. The dolmans are cut to fit the figure more tightly, the waistline is set lower and the braid and bobbin lace trimmings are superseded by Rococo-style floral embroidery.

89 LADY'S EVENING DRESS

Inv. No.: 1958.369.1–2. Silk, woven
Length of bodice: 36 cm, length of skirt: 115 cm, waist: 66 cm
1893

Worn by Mrs. Jakab Mattyasovszky, née Teréz Zsolnay, daughter of the founder of the famous Zsolnay porcelain factory, on the occasion of the opening of the Pécs National Theatre in 1893.

Made of *chiné* silk with a pattern of vertical green satin stripes alternating with a vertical meandering design of red carnations with green stalks against a white background. The V-shaped neckline is cut on the bias thus emphasizing the design of the silk. The waistline curves downwards but is concealed by a folded belt which fastens in front with hooks. The huge puffed sleeves are gathered into the shoulder and at the elbows. The flared skirt consists of several panels and the train at the back is gathered into a fan-shape at the back of the waist.

This gown, worn as full evening dress, is an example of how Viennese fashion introduced French prototypes to Hungary.

90 LADY'S EVENING GOWN

Inv. No.: T. 1972.222.1–2. Embroidered silk with a tulle skirt
Length of skirt: 102 cm, length of bodice: 44 cm, waist: 65 cm
1937

Its owner, a member of the Palestrina Choir, wore this gown on a concert tour of Italy in 1937.

The bodice is of black silk with *matyó* embroidery worked in coloured wools in a pattern of flowers and hearts, which runs from the shoulders covering the bust-seams in front and over the vertical seams at the back. The open V of the front is laced up with a woollen cord twisted from several shades of red. The edges of the bodice are bound with red velvet. The full sleeves of black tulle which reach to below the elbow are also bound with red velvet. The skirt, too, is made of black tulle; of circular cut it is gathered into the waistline to fall in folds. The gown, designed to be worn on festive occasions, is a particularly fine example of a dress which, while distantly following the European high fashion, still retains its Hungarian character by its use of folk motifs embroidered in wool.

91 BACKGAMMON BOARD

Inv. No.: 1972.114. Silver and silver-gilt with enamel and precious stones
Length: 39.5 cm, width: 31.5 cm, height: 15.5 cm
17th century

The backgammon is said to have belonged to Mihály Apafi I (1632–1690), Prince of Transylvania. It has not been possible to corroborate this assumption so far although a 'large-sized backgammon' does figure in the 1724 inventory of the estate of the Prince's daughter-in-law, the Countess Kata Bethlen. The wooden book-shaped box is covered with silver both inside and out. The four sides are covered with a leaf and flower design in Transylvanian enamel, also both inside and out. In the centre of the outside of each half of the board is a large polished oval agate, held in a silver-gilt mount. Round the large agates are 28 small agates and bloodstones of various shapes embedded in wreaths of black enamel petals, arranged in a formal pattern. Each half of the board has a broad band set with 14 flat-cut agates as a border; the agates measure 6.7×5.3 cm and are separated from each other by tiny cast silver flowers and rosettes in high relief. On the four sides of the board are 36 agates of a similar size also set among small cast flowers and rosettes. Inside, the playing surface of the board is covered with silver filigree work. The acute-angled triangles with rounded ends—the so-called 'points'—are of silver alternating with gold and are set with their tips facing each other. The 12 small plates run down each side. The dividing line between the two sides is composed of three horizontally placed oval agates and the same number of blood-stones.

92 COVERED TANKARD

Inv. No.: 1973.33. Silver-gilt with silver decoration
Height: 26 cm, diameter of foot: 13.2 cm
c. 1670

The tankard came to the Hungarian National Museum bequested by József Teleki. There is no evidence, however, to show that it had always belonged to the Teleki family or was made for them.

The circular articulated foot is decorated with an attached border of pierced flowers and leaves in relief. The plain cylindrical drum is encased in a silver casting, pierced and in high relief, portraying a scene of oriental merchants. The lid is surrounded by a wreath of flowers and leaves; the knob is formed by the figure of a Roman warrior leaning on a shield which bears the initials M. T. in small letters. The handle is cast and embossed in the shape of a Baroque herm.

The Museum's collection includes several jewel trays worked in repoussé with scenic decorations and fruit and flowers, executed by Mihály Allert of Besztercebánya (Banská Bystrica). The techniques used in the making of this tankard place it among the Upper Hungarian goldsmiths' works of the seventeenth century.

93 COVERED GOBLET

Inv. No.: 1901.115. Silver and parcel gilt
Height: 26.5 cm
1729

The bowl, tapering towards the foot, and the foot itself are both divided by sharp ribs into four flat and four convex fields, decorated in two engraved repoussé interlaced ribbon patterns which alternate. The corresponding fields on the lid, which is also octagonal with several articulations, are decorated in the same way. The knob in the centre of the lid is in the form of a bud rising among leaves. The rim of the lid is engraved with the inscription: GROF BETHLEN KLARA (Countess Klara Bethlen). The detachable foot is inscribed Ge. May 1 1729. Many of the products from the goldsmiths' workshops show marked changes in design in the first decades of the eighteenth century. Goldsmiths of Brassó (Brașov) developed these new six or eight-sided cups with flat ornamentation, a style based on the pattern-books they had acquired during their years of travel. We owe the finest examples of these cups to the goldsmiths of the May dynasty.

The goblet was made for the daughter of János Bethlen who married Pál Mikó in 1728. It was purchased by the National Museum.

94 JEWELLERY TO BE WORN WITH FULL DRESS

Inv. No.: 1971.29.1–6. Gold, cast and engraved

Belt length: 83 cm, width 5.5 cm, diameter of clasp: 7 cm, chain for fastening the *mente*, length: 36 cm, width: 5 cm, clasp, diameter: 7 cm, plumes of aigrette, length: 15 cm, width: 7.5 cm, rosette of aigrette, diameter: 5 cm, sword suspension, length: 28 cm and 56 cm, set of 24 buttons, diameter: 2 cm and 1.5 cm, set of 28 buttons, length: 3.4, 3.2 and 2 cm, diameter 1.9, 1.7 and 1.7 cm respectively.

7th and 16th centuries and the 1860s

The pieces of jewellery dating from the Migration Period and the chain dating from the 16th century came into the possession of the Patay family who had them refashioned as a part of a set of jewellery to be worn with a man's full dress in the sixties of the last century. The set was purchased by the Hungarian National Museum.

THE BELT: the round clasp in the middle, with a centrally mounted topaz, was originally a pectoral ornament dating from the Migration Period. Round the topaz are pearls, gold granules and concentric circles of gold open-work. The belt proper, into which the clasp is set, is made up of sixteenth-century interlocked elements of Renaissance design, known to Hungarians as the 'nut-kernel' pattern. At each end is a curved band decorated with a row of very small gold beads.

THE FASTENING OF THE MENTE was made as a copy of the belt in the sixties of the nineteenth century. A large topaz is set in the middle of the round clasp, in which the circles of gold open-work are substituted by Neo-Gothic pierced decoration. The rest of the fastening is identical in design with the belt but the 'nut-kernel' chain does not date from the sixteenth century—it is a copy.

AIGRETTE: the topaz in the centre of the rosette has a claw setting but is otherwise similar to the clasp of the *mente* fastening. Three plumes, their fronds shaped like ears of corn, branch out from the rosette.

SWORD SUSPENSIONS: 2 pieces. Formed from the original Renaissance 'nut-kernel' chain separated and joined by an oval ring between each link.

SET OF 24 BUTTONS: dating from the 1860s. Cut topaz in gold mounts decorated with minute flowers and a netted pattern.

SET OF 28 BUTTONS: silver-gilt in three sizes for the fastenings of the *dolman* (jacket), the *mente* and the sleeves. The buttons for the dolman and the sleeves were made in Pest in 1818; those for the *mente* were copied from them in the 1860s. The buttons are egg-shaped, their surface is decorated with twisted fluting, the grooves of which are filled in with twisted wire. The single Baroque pearl on the top of each button is held by an eight-petalled gold circle surrounded by a row of beading.

The earliest piece in the set—the one which dates from the Migration Period—is the round central clasp of the belt, to which the sixteenth-century 'nut-kernel' chain is attached. According to family tradition the chain belonged to Mihály Teleki II, Chancellor of Transylvania.

214

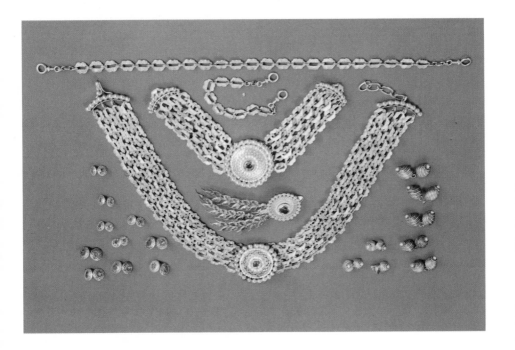

95 'IVORY' SADDLES (Detail)

Inv. No.: 55.3117; 55.3118; 55.3119. Bone and wood, carved
Lengths: 54, 56 and 56 cm respectively
Early 15th century

The first saddle was donated to the Hungarian National Museum by János Zichy, the second by Lajos Rhédey; the third found its way to the Museum from the Jankovich Collection.

The finest relics of knightly equipment from the Middle Ages are those which date from the reign of the Emperor Sigismund, King of Hungary. Only 21 pieces have survived of which three are preserved in the Hungarian National Museum. The pommels and sides of these saddles are profusely decorated with a splendid variety of characters and scenes, carved in relief.

The first saddle is carved with scenes from the life of St. George, and show him killing the dragon as the Princess kneels beside him. An angel, whose naked body is covered by a flimsy veil, holds a banderole with the inscription: DA PACEM DOMINE (Give us peace, O Lord!). This saddle was produced in 1430 and the others with which we are familiar were made at about the same time. Only a few of them follow the normal western pattern of tournament saddles, they are more usually characterized by a low rear pommel, bending backwards and cut in a heart-shape. The earliest specimen of this type of saddle can be seen on the statue of St. George made by Márton and György Kolozsvári in 1373. It is assumed that the saddles preserved in the Museum are the work of Rhenish master-craftsmen, commissioned by the sumptuous Emperor Sigismund and presented by him to members of his Order of the Dragon. Fantastic scenes of the courtly ove of the Middle Ages; the unicorn, the wild man (wodewoser) with a halberd, the masked man fighting with a lion, deer and dragons were often carved on these saddles.

The second saddle portrays two lovers in an amorous scene, a youth playing a musical nstrument, semi-naked figures and a huntsman sticking a wild boar. Both profane and religious subjects figure strangely together in these carvings.

St. George appears again on the third saddle, together with naked figures, apes and dragons. In the background Phyllis is represented riding on the back of Aristotle, who is holding a scroll with the inscription, "Laugh, my dear, laugh!" The scenes on the saddles can be explained by German love poems. In this interpretation St. George always holds the key position while animals—lions, gryphons, dragons, unicorns and apes represent the virtues or the passions symbolically employed by the poets.

216

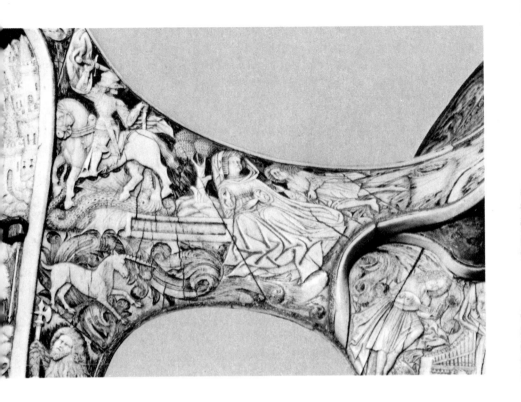

96 ORNAMENTAL PAPAL SWORD OF KING WLADISLAS II

Inv. No.: 55.3235. Silver and enamelled iron; forged steel blade; the belt of silk
Lengths: blade: 168 cm, sheath: 112.4 cm, cross-bar: 43 cm
1509

This sword first appeared in the inventory drawn up at the famous Castle of Ambras after the death of the Archduke Ferdinand of Tyrol on May 30, 1596. After many vicissitudes it was returned to Hungary under the terms of arbitration held in Venice on November 27, 1932.

The weapon, one of the outstanding pieces of the crafts of Italian Renaissance silversmiths, was made in 1509 by Domenico de Sutrio. The handguard is of richly chased silver-gilt. The hilt terminates in a large silver-gilt knob; its enamel decoration, which includes the della Rovere coat of arms painted in gold, is now badly worn.

The sheath is gold-plated beaten silver with a pierced decoration. Masks, dolphins and grotesques, alternating among acanthus leaves, are a demonstration of a masterly sense of composition. The papal della Rovere arms appear again at the end of the sheath on a slightly convex enamelled plate produced, apparently, by two different techniques; the lower half is niello, the upper half is of champlevé enamel work. The use of two different enamelling techniques on one small area is in itself a proof of the masterly skill and inventiveness which characterizes the silversmith work on this ornamental sword.

The gold brocade sword-belt is a masterpiece too. Its design is composed of three motifs: the della Rovere arms, the papal tiara with the crossed keys of St. Peter and the foliage which connects the two heraldic devices. The shield which forms the field of the coat of arms is of blue silk. The belt is the work of Bernardo Ser Silvano, whose name as well as that of Pietro Mancino, the maker of the hilt, are known to us from the 1509 accounts of the papal treasury.

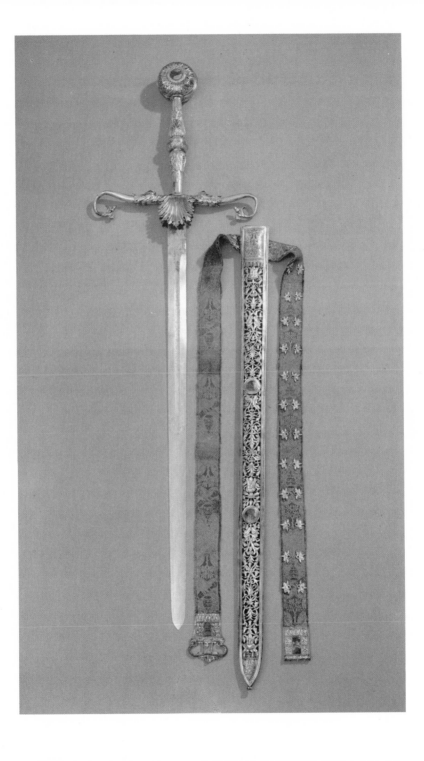

97 SUIT OF ARMOUR OF LOUIS II, KING OF HUNGARY

Inv. No.: 55.3269. Wrought iron, silver-plated
Height: 157 cm
Beginning of the 16th century

The armour was returned to Hungary under the terms of the decision arrived a tthrough arbitration in Venice, on November 27, 1932. It is believed to have been a gift to the nine-year-old Louis, undeveloped for his age, from the Emperor Maximilian on July 23, 1515.

This suit of armour of Louis II was already described in the first catalogue of Tyrolian weapons as the finest item in the collection.

The most peculiar feature of the armour is the close-helmet, composed of six separate pieces, which is so accurate in its construction and decoration that it appears to be a structural part of the armour itself. The decorative lozenges on both the armour and the helmet are each filled with an embossed, etched and finally gilt quatrefoil design, an imitation of the slashed ornamentation of the *Landsknecht* costume, which was constructed of square or lozenge-shaped pieces of cloth, each slashed in a conventional design to allow a linen or coloured silk shirt peeping through the slits.

The shoes belonging to this armour differ from the peaked ones typical of the period of Maximilian, with their broad toes they follow the *Landsknecht* fashion of the period. The armour's edges are decorated with a roped border and an etched and gilt stripe imitating embroidery. On the breastplate is a woman's head similar to the *Jungfrauenadler* figure which appears in one field of the triple arms of the city of Nuremberg. It may, therefore, be presumed that the suit of armour was produced in that city. The initials E. S., also on the breast and executed in the same technique as the rest of the ornament, are of special interest. The same two letters appear on the front and back pommels of the steel saddle belonging to the armour. Some scholars associate them with the name of St. Elizabeth, daughter of King András II; others see in them the initials of the armourer

98 SÁMUEL TELEKI'S SADDLE

Inv. No.: 55.7789. Wood and silver with enamel work
Height: 44 cm, height of pommel: 30 cm
17th century

From the Teleki Collection.
The saddle of a nobleman. Produced under eastern influence, the plain silver-gilt plate which forms the basic covering of the frame can hardly be seen for the mass of dazzling jewels and magnificent cloisonné enamel with which it is decorated. The actual surface of the saddle is covered by silver filigree and a complicated pattern of charmingly disposed flowers in Hungarian cloisonné enamel on a silver ground. The borders of the pommel and the framework of the saddle are decorated with a line of particles of blue enamel which in their turn are edged with a line of rubies and emeralds, set in raised mounts. The surface of the pommel is ornamented with three large Persian 'pears' and three small rosettes, set with rubies and emeralds. The jewels compete in splendour with the enamel work; the metal covering of the saddle was so highly elaborated by the silversmith that no less than 597 precious stones stand in relief against their background of cloisonné enamel. On those parts which are gilded, the floral pattern in white, green, pale blue and yellow reflects eastern decoration. The scrolls of wire surrounding the precious stones terminate in dark leaves, buds and full-blown carnations and tulips while, perched on some of the petals, are small silver birds. The red velvet seat is covered by carnations and tulips embroidered in gold.

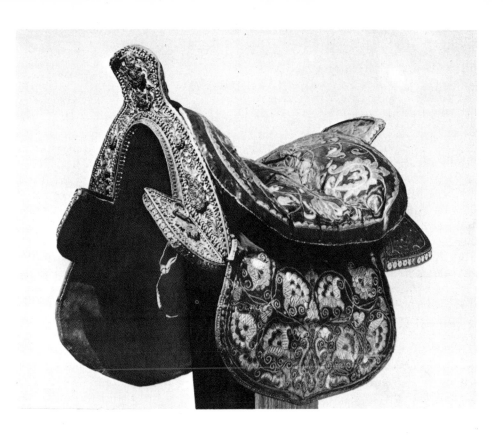

99 BROADSWORD AND SABRE OF JÁNOS KEMÉNY, PRINCE OF TRANSYLVANIA

Inv. No.: 55.3345 and 55.3344. Forged steel and enamelled silver
Length: 105 and 97 cm, width: 2.7 and 3.5 cm respectively
17th century

Acquired by the Hungarian National Museum in 1832 from the Jankovich Collection. The broadsword of János Kemény was thought for a long time to have belonged to István Báthori, Prince of Transylvania and King of Poland. Both its sheath and its hilt are decorated with cloisonné enamel and so is the sheath of the sabre, which comes from the same workshop, and is inscribed with the name János Kemény. The design of the flowers and the colouring of the enamel on the two weapons are so similar that they must be regarded as belonging together. The enamel plaques on the sheath of the sabre are slightly larger but on both sets of plaques the enamel work is heightened by the addition of turquoises and gold granulation. The blade of the sabre is stamped with a crescent-shaped swordsmith mark; the blade of the broadsword bears the word *Genova* and nine jug-shaped armourers' marks. The enamel decoration on both the broadsword and the sabre belongs unquestionably to the well-defined and circumscribed category of Transylvanian enamelling. Both weapons are characterized by the wires applied to the edges; on the flat of the blades are almond-shaped cartouches, a technique that was often used on dress-swords and goldsmiths' works of the sixteenth century. The great demand for dress-swords and other objects in precious metals induced goldsmiths to make the objects they produced look striking and attractive even if they were actually thought of as of lesser value. They hoped, by the skilful use of enamelling and filigree work, to achieve quick results which demanded comparatively small quantities of precious metal.

100 POWDER-HORNS

Inv. No.: 53.1177, 53.1235. Carved stag's horn
Height: 32.5 cm and 31.5 cm, width: 22.5 cm and 21 cm respectively
Beginning of the 18th century

The first specimen came to the Hungarian National Museum in 1859 from the Kehrer Collection; the second, bearing the name Ábrahám Zolnay, was bought by the Museum in 1889.

The powder-horns, cut from antlers, are ornamented with the arms of the Zolnay family; both are three-branched and closely covered with engravings of hunting scenes. The first horn is inscribed with the name Sándor Zolnay, it has a carved measuring device and iron suspension loops. On the second horn a scene of bear-hunting is engraved, as well as various birds and other animals, and, in addition, the Zolnay coat of arms. At the end of the branches is a geometrical ornamental border. The coat of arms and the drawing of the animals is of somewhat uncertain workmanship but in handling the stylized floral decoration the maker rose to a high artistic level. The measuring device on the second horn is of more recent date.

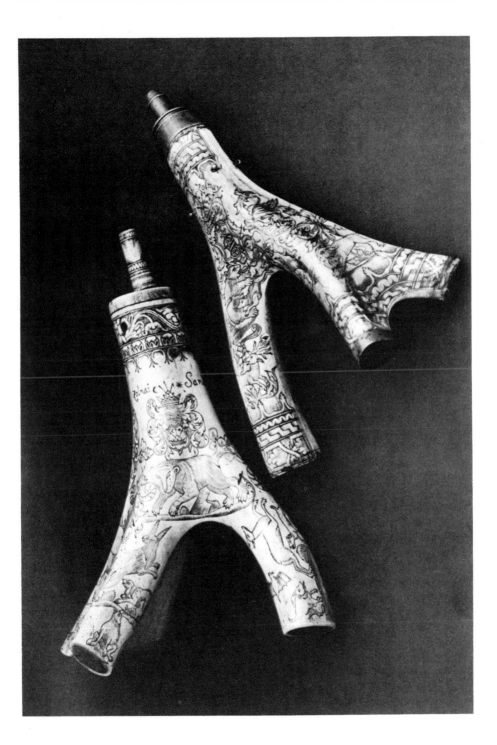

101 GUN AND ATTACHMENTS, IN A CASE

Inv. No.: 56.5262. Damascened steel and ivory
Length: 83 cm, width: 22 cm
19th century

The gun in its case was returned to Hungary by the terms of the arbitration conducted in Venice on November 27, 1932.

The gun was made by the famous Hungarian gunsmith, József Kirner, for the Crown Prince Rudolf. It is recognized throughout the world as a supreme masterpiece of the gunsmith's craft and has been exhibited on several occasions at world fairs. Weapons made by Kirner bear witness to the high standards that can be reached in works of craftsmanship when talent and energy are united. Kirner devoted special attention to the exquisite gold-inlaid engravings he used as ornamentation; his dedication, engraved on the keyhole cover, reads: "To His Imperial and Royal Majesty, the Crown Prince RUDOLF, commended with the deepest homage by József Kirner, gunsmith to the Royal Court of Hungary".

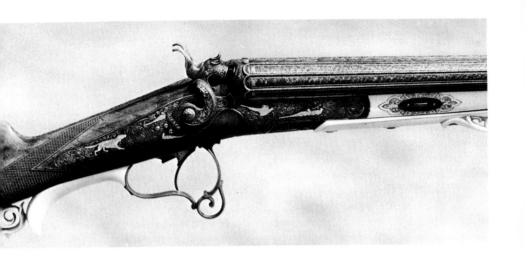

M. KIR. UDVARI
KIRNER JOSEF PESTEN
FEGYVERGYÁROS

102 CUPBOARD

Inv. No.: 1954.472. Walnut, carved, with yew and maple marquetry
Height: 260 cm, width: 180 cm, depth: 64 cm
c. 1700

A large two-door cupboard veneered in walnut on a walnut carcass, with canted corners and supported on bun-feet beneath an undulating base. Each of the two doors is divided into two major panels surrounded by elaborate mouldings within which are designs composed of naturalistic birds, butterflies, insects, apes and lions, executed in marquetry. The pediment of the cupboard consists of foliated scrolls which run in either direction from a square central inlaid ornament.

Stylistically the cupboard combines two different periods. The carved cornice still reveals marks of seventeenth-century taste while the rich marquetry is characteristic of the eighteenth century. Because the cupboard had belonged to the Rosos family of Szentkirályszabadja, it may be assumed that this outstandingly beautiful specimen of Baroque furniture was produced in the Transdanubian region of Hungary at the beginning of the eighteenth century.

103 WRITING CABINET

Inv. No.: 1954.470. Walnut with marquetry
Height: 178 cm, width: 162 cm
First half of the 18th century

This robust writing cabinet has a walnut veneering with a very rich, light-coloured ribbon intarsia in a symmetrical composition. It is divided into three parts: the lower one consisting of three drawers of a curved profile, the sloping central portion closed by a flap and the superimposed cabinet of an introflexed shape. This latter embraces a central cupboard flanked by five small drawers each. The pediment of the lower section is voluted, the crowning pediment arched.

The noble simplicity of this cabinet places it among the finest pieces of Transylvanian furniture to come down to us. It is believed to have been a product of the highly organized Nagyszeben (Sibiu) furniture-making industry.

104 ARMCHAIR

Inv. No.: 1967.89. Carved lime-wood
Height: 121 cm, width: 78.5 cm, depth: 45 cm
Between 1720 and 1735

The lime-wood armchair we see here is a highly valued historic relic, carved by Ferenc Rákóczi II (1676–1735), Prince of Transylvania and leader of the *kuruc* fight for freedom, during his exile in Rodostó (Tekirdag, Turkey). He designed the chair for his own use in the chapel there; it was discovered by Kálmán Thaly who brought it back after he had been to search for the Prince's mortal remains. It was taken first to Kassa (Košice) and later found its way to the Hungarian National Museum.

The cabriole legs, the front of the seat and the straight high back are profusely decorated with carved flowers and leaves, the stretchers are boldly curved. The elaborately pierced splat is surmounted by a small cartouche enclosing a small painted rose, above it the back is carved with clusters of flowers and fruit; bunches of grapes hang down on the two sides. The arms curve outwards, the trapezoidal seat is covered in hard leather. The armchair is painted in pink, green and blue on a white ground.

105 GUILD CHEST

Inv. No.: 1950.5. Maple inlaid with poplar root
Length: 64.5 cm, width: 41 cm, height: 54 cm
First half of the 19th century

The chest was deposited in the Museum by the Stone-masons Trade Association of Budapest; it is probable, therefore, that it belonged formerly to the Pest guild of stone-masons.

The oblong chest is in the form of a classical peristyle temple with a tympanum on the front side decorated with symbols of masonry in copper. The carcass behind the pediment has a plain top which can be lifted on two side-rails; its lock is opened by three keys. The keyholes are covered by silver escutcheons. In the interior is a small drawer at each side. Along the bottom of the chest, below the columns, is a large drawer with silver knobs; the carcass behind the columns is rusticated. The whole chest is made of maple inlaid with poplar root banded with ash.

106 JUG

Inv. No.: 1961.404. Tin-glazed faience
Height: 20 cm
1679

An egg-shaped Habán ewer with a fluted body, compared to which the straight neck is rather short. The handle springs from the lower part of the neck and curves gently outwards to end about half-way down the swelling body. The decoration in white tin-glaze is symmetrically arranged; the flowers in the middle of the bouquet are ochre and blue, the leaves green and the outlines of the design manganese brown. The figures of the date when the jug was made are painted on either side of the bouquet, 16 on the left and 79 on the right. Between the date and the handle, on each side of the jug, is a small spray of flowers and leaves.

107 DISH

Inv. No.: 1954.436. Tin-glazed faience
Diameter: 31 cm
1692

A broad-rimmed Habán dish with floral decoration on a white ground. On the rim, at equal distances apart, are three sprays each composed of two tulips and three leaves, together with the date: 1692. In the round hollow of the dish, surrounded by two blue stripes are three tulips and above them the initials P. H. The typically Habán decoration is in blue, yellow, purple and green.

238

108 SPICE JAR

Inv. No.: 1939.61. Tin-glazed faience
Height: 23 cm
1670

Octagonal Habán spice jar with a very small lid. Each of the eight sides of the jar is ornamented with a typically Habán design of flowers and foliage. The neck of the jar bears the following abbreviated inscription in capital letters: "GE(nerosus) DO(minus) NI(colaus) IA(klin) DE EL(efánt) 1670", identifying the owner of the jar, Miklós Jaklin of Elefánt, Castellan of Léva (Levice). The tin screw-cap is provided with a late Renaissance handle engraved with the letters A. G. The colouring—ochre, blue, green and purple—is extremely harmonious.

109 ROUND DISH

Inv. No.: 1961.440. Tin-glazed faience
Diameter: 35 cm
1693

A large white Habán dish, characterized by the fine body and the high-gloss of its milk-white tin-glaze, usual in vessels of this type. Its decoration consists of a floral design in Renaissance style, in which three floral sprays of tulips and pomegranates are evenly distributed round the rim, whose inner edge is surrounded by a painted lace pattern. In the hollow centre of the dish the initials M P, and below them the date, are surrounded by a wreath of green leaves. The colours are those usually to be found on white-based Habán ware—ochre, purple, cobalt blue and green.

110 JUG

Inv. No.: 54.414. Tin-glazed faience
Height: 19.5 cm
Late 17th, early 18th century

A Habán jug with a tin lid and base. Round the neck and one-third of the way down the bulging round belly, set between two borders, each of two narrow parallel blue stripes, the jug is decorated with a floral design in which the tulip is the main motif. The date 1699 appears on either side of the handle, two figures on each side: 16–99. Among the strong colours purple is dominant. The tin lid was executed at a later date, and it bears the initials H. C. W. and the year 1717.

111 FLASKS
Inv. No.: 1913.104.4.5. Blown glass decorated with painting in enamels
Height; 19 cm
Second half of the 18th century

Small size brandy flasks, made, presumably, in one of the Transdanubian glass-works. In shape they resemble prisms, with chamfered edges, the neck is rounded. The decoration is carried out in red, yellow, blue, green, white and black enamel paint. The broad sides of each flask—opposite each other—are painted with branching floral designs, the narrower sides each with a single flower, while the chamfered sections are ornamented with motifs reminiscent of Baroque calligraphy. The tin screw caps of both flasks are incomplete.

112 FLOWER BOWL WITH PERFORATED COVER

Inv. No.: 1961.1660.1–2. Tin-glazed faience
Height: 20.5 cm
End of the 18th century

The white bowl with its lightly fluted round belly is a product of the Holics factory founded in 1743. On the upper part of every second plane there is a small hole, each designed to hold a single flower. The lid, the centre of which is a hemisphere, is pierced with semicircular holes of larger size. The body of the pot is covered by coloured branches of flowers, modelled in high relief. The violet and yellow flowers, green leaves and brown branches produce a charmingly balanced decoration. A twisting branch which curls round the cover rises up to make a small handle by which it can be lifted.

113 FISH-SERVER

Inv. No.: 1962.89. Porcelain
Length: 72 cm, width: 25.6 cm
1842

The fish-server is said to have been made for the first exhibition of industrial art in Hungary.

It is a long oval dish with an undulating edge and decoration both inside and out with strikingly contrasted patterns. On the inside the dish is entirely covered by delicately painted ornamental flowers and leaves on finely drawn branches which run in parallel lines along the length of the dish. The stems of the foliage are cyclamen-colour and most of the narrow leaves gold, interspersed with a few which are green. At equally spaced intervals are red flowers with golden centres and between them smaller flowers in dark blue and cyclamen pink. The gilt-edged border of the dish is sparsely decorated with delicate gold twigs. The reverse of the dish has, in its centre, a very large highly naturalistic representation of a tree in full-leaf, against a pale blue background. An extremely complicated stripe consisting of flowers and leaves, resembling, and presumably based on, a textile pattern runs round the reverse border of the dish. Below and above the tree at the two ends of the dish, within three white stripes, is the following impressed mark:

    FISCHER MORICZ
      HERENDEN
        842

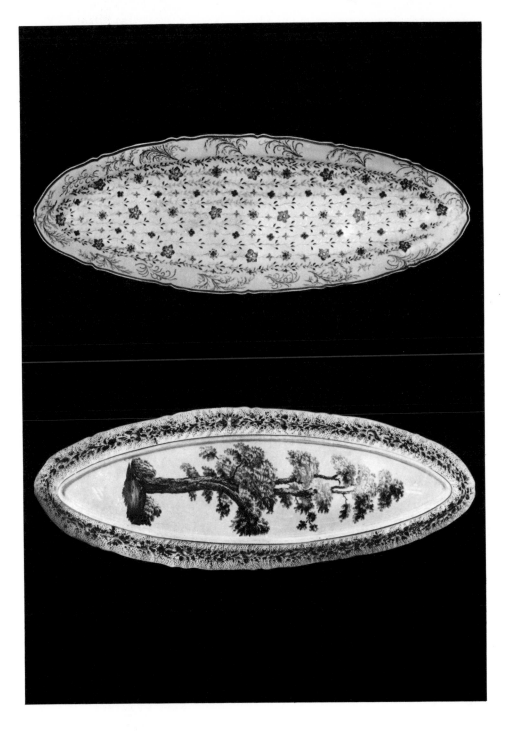

114 VIRGINAL

Inv. No.: App. Jank. 243. Ebony with silver-gilt and enamel plaques
Height: 25 cm, width: 43 cm, depth: 23.5 cm
First quarter of the 17th century

According to tradition, before this virginal found its way to the Hungarian National Museum's collection of musical instruments, it belonged to Catherine of Brandenburg, second wife of Gábor Bethlen, Prince of Transylvania.

The case is ebony, on its sloping lid a velvet cushion. On the whole of the outside and part of the inside are attached plaques of silver, silver-gilt and enamel; a striking feature of the instrument when it is open is a series of pictures on the lid enclosed in hexagonal and octagonal frames, representing the four senses—touch, taste, smell and sound. On the inner side of the case are scenes from the Bible in painted enamel; between them is the year when the instrument was made and the maker's mark. Groups of people playing musical instruments appear in other scenes and above the keyboard can be read: OMNIS. SPIRITVS. LAVDET. DOMINVM. (and) SIC. TRANSIT. GLORIAE. MVNDI.

This sort of keyboard instruments of the period was greatly favoured by young girls. The keyboard of the virginal stretches from F to g^2 (three octaves and a second).

The original mechanism of the virginal, sounded by plucking the strings, was replaced at the beginning of the nineteenth century by the present overstrung German structure and a new sounding case.

252

115 CEMBALO

Inv. No.: 1847.30. Painted pine
Height: 18 cm, length: 172 cm, width: 73.5 cm
17th century

The greater part of this single-manual clavicembalo—the body, the top and the sounding board—is made of pine; only the moving parts, exposed to heavier wear, are made of the harder maple or beech; pear-wood is used for the parts which show, a beautiful wood and easy to work, but still having the necessary hardness.

The sides of the case, reinforced on the outside by small wooden panels, are decorated with painted marbling on a green ground; the lid is painted in irregular patches of blue and red on a ground of the same colours but paler; the patches are outlined with a fine black line. The flowers on the sounding board are painted in naive or 'popular' style, the additional gilding, the red and blue pattern on the inner sides give this clavicembalo a particular interest.

The keyboard itself is supported on either side by low walls carved in an unusual manner, and above the keyboard are the painted arms of the Thököly family and an inscription: COMES STEPHANUS THÖKÖLI

de Kés-marck

The structure of this instrument is typical of the seventeenth-century cembali; the only innovation lies in the S-shape of the key stem by which the measurable distance between two strings was reduced to about one-third as compared to that of other cembalos.

The instrument is provided with two eight-foot stringlines and one lute variant probably added later.

The maker of this cembalo is not known. Its construction points to Italian influence while its decoration and the wood of which it is made suggest that it comes from Hungary.

116 BARYTONE

Inv. No.: 1949.360. Maple and pine-wood
Height: 60 cm, width on top: 30 cm, at bottom: 37 cm
1750

The belly of the instrument is lacquered in pale yellow, its back and sides are decorated with undulating lines of marquetry. The supplementary fingerboard, covering the lower strings, is ornamented with a delicate design of curling foliage and the letters I. S.—the initials of the maker. Instead of terminating in the usual spiral this is replaced at the head of the instrument by the carved head of a man wearing a cap of Hungarian style. The barytone has seven strings for playing with a bow and ten to be plucked. Inside the belly a printed label bears the signature "Joann Joseph Stadlmann Kaiserl. königl. Hof Lauten-und Geigenmacher in Wienn 1750".

The barytone is one of the most difficult instruments to manipulate. In essentials it is like a viola da gamba but, in addition to its several strings to be played with a bow, resonant chords can be plucked under the fingerboard with the thumb of the left hand.

The special value and interest of the instrument in the Museum's collection lies in its historical associations. It belonged once to (and perhaps was even made for) Prince Miklós Esterházy at Kismarton (Eisenstadt) and later at Eszterháza (Fertőd) Castle where Joseph Haydn composed about 150 pieces of music for his aristocratic employer, destined to be performed on this rare and beautiful instrument. The case made to hold it also survives.

117 HARP

Inv. No.: 1852.65. Pine and maple-wood, gilded
Height: 150 cm, width: 80 cm, breadth: 30 cm
Second half of the 18th century

Both convincing data and tradition point to Marie Antoinette as having played on this harp who made a present of the instrument to the Countess Benyovszky, wife of the "King of Madagascar", through whom it found its way to Hungary and eventually to the National Museum.

The carved and gilded floral festoons which cover the pillar, the part of the base that is gilded and the rounded outer side of the sound-body seem, as it were, to embrace the mythological scenes painted in a masterly manner on the flat face of the sound-body. The paintings represent an amorous episode between Venus and Mars; Vulcan's forge in the background and a small cupid playing with the helmet of Mars in the foreground.

With its 35 strings and its 7 pedals set into slots in its base, this harp already approaches, in its design, the so-called E-flat major type of instrument in use today. Compared to the more primitive 'hooked' types the great merit of the pedal-operated harp was that it lessened the strain on the hands. The value of this particular instrument is increased by the fact that its maker, Pierre-Joseph Cousineau, was instrument-maker to the Queen and, at the same time, the first master of the craft to elaborate further the pedal movement.

118 PIANOFORTE

Inv. No.: 1887.41.29. (Liszt bequest.) Mahogany
Width: 115 cm, length: 247 cm, height: 92 cm
1818

This pianoforte was sent from London to Vienna in 1818 as a gift to Beethoven from its makers. After his death in 1827 it was sold by auction and its whereabouts remained unknown for some years. In about 1840 it came into the possession of Ferenc Liszt, who left the famous instrument in his will to the Hungarian National Museum.

The case of this late Georgian piano is mahogany; above the keyboard is the name and address of the makers: JOHN BROADWOOD AND SONS (Maker to his Majesty and the Princesses) Great Pulteney Street LONDON Golden Square, above is the name BEETHOVEN, the whole in gold letters framed by an inlaid decoration. There is, in addition, level with the wrest-block, an inscription in Latin which reads: "Hoc Instrumentum est Thomae Broadwood (londini) donum propter ingenium illustrissimi Beethoven". Beside it are the signatures of the committee entrusted with the choosing of the instrument: Fr. Kalkbrenner (subsequently erased), Ferd. Ries, J. B. Cramer, J. G. Ferrari, C. Knyvett.

The compass of the keyboard covers six octaves—C_1 to c^4. The strings are three to a note throughout.

119 POCKET WATCH

Inv. No.: App. Jank. 80. Copper gilt
Length: 8 cm, width: 6 cm, height: 3.2 cm
Turn of the 16th–17th centuries

The watch belongs to the first group of antiques from the collection of Miklós Janko-vich which came to the National Museum as early as the 1830s.

The copper watch-case is made up of several parts separately cast and then soldered together. The pierced cover has, in the centre, the coat of arms of the Báthori family, decorated with the collar and pendant of the Order of the Golden Fleece. Zsigmond Báthori (1572–1613) was the member of the family to be created prince and invested with the Order of the Golden Fleece in 1597. It can be assumed, therefore, that the watch was made between 1597 and 1614 in Transylvania.

The works, which are driven by a mainspring, include both a striking and an alarm mechanism. The escapement is now regulated by a spiral balance which must have been put into the watch between 1675 and 1720. The dial is graded I–XII; it may be inferred from the fact that there is only one hand that the watch was unlikely to have been used very long after 1700.

120 SEAL

Inv. No.: Cim. Sec. I.V.3. Bronze-gilt, engraved
Diameter of seal: 7.1 cm, diameter including loops: 9.4 cm
Between 1202–1255

A circular double-sided seal with four attached metal loops projecting at equal distances; once the seal of the Esztergom 'Latins'. In the centre of the obverse of the seal is the engraved representation of a large group of buildings consisting of a central tower and two identical wings; all three buildings have tiled roofs and tracery windows. The buildings are surrounded by a crenelated wall with bastions, four of which can be seen. In the middle of the wall is an ornate gateway in which is set a door with fittings; smaller doors are set into the walls to the left and to the right of the main gateway. The legend, in Gothic capitals, reads: SIGILLVM LATINORVM CIVITATIS STRIGO-NIENSIS.

The reverse of the seal bears a shield of barry of nine pieces and the legend—also in Gothic capitals—reads: SECRETVM LATINORVM CIVITATIS STRIGONI-ENSIS.

The term 'Latin' appears in Hungarian documents to denote those settlers who came from Northern France, Flanders, Spain and Italy and spoke Romance language. They played an important part in the development of Hungarian towns as well as in the organization of the country's trade. Esztergom was one of their most important centres and also, for a long time, a place of royal residence.

The first wax impression of this seal to have come down to us is from the year 1269.

121 SEAL

Inv. No.: Cim. Sec. I.V.4. Engraved silver
Diameter: 5.3–6.1 cm
14th century

The seal of the town of Újbánya (Nová Baňa), Czechoslovakia.
A hexagonal seal; on the obverse is engraved a representation of the Madonna and Child enthroned. The Child, who stands on his Mother's knee, stretches out his arm in blessing over the head of King Louis I (1342–1382), who kneels before the throne, offering up his crown. A banderole floating behind the king bears the inscription: LVDOWICuS. The seal itself has a border with the legend: +SIGILLVM · CIVITATIS · DE · MONTE REGIS.

122 GOLD SEAL

Inv. No.: 1881.26. Gold
Diameter: 6.7 cm
13th century

Round seal of Béla IV, King of Hungary (1235–1270), during whose reign the country was devastated by the Mongol invaders; the King himself was pursued as far as Dalmatia. Following his return, Béla IV devoted most of his reign to the reparation of the ravage caused by the Mongols and made every effort to build up the country once more.

The relief on the obverse of the seal shows the King enthroned, crowned and holding in his right hand the sceptre and in his left the orb. The legend surrounding the image of the King reads: +BELA · DeI · GRATia · HVNGaRie DALMACie · CROHaCie · RAMe · SerVIE · GALICie · LODOMerie · CVMAnIe · REX. On the reverse, in an escutcheon, a double cross in relief with the legend: +SIGILLVM · QVARTI · BELE · SECVNDI · ANDREE · REGIS · FILII.

123 SEAL

Inv. No.: 1873.262. Silver, engraved
Diameter: 6.3 cm, height: 15 cm
The last years of the 17th century

A large seal on a prism-shaped iron tang. The seal itself is engraved on a silver plate. In the centre the arms of the Rákóczi family of Rákócz and Felsővadász: the shield party per fesse, in the top half an eagle displayed, holding a drawn sabre in its left claws; in the lower half a wheel over a tripartite mound; with a mantle made of ermine and the princely crown.

The seal is bordered by a laurel-wreath within which are two lines of inscription which run: FRANCISCVS DEI GRATIA PRINC(eps) RAKOCZI COMES DE SAAROS DVX MVNKACSIE ET MAKOVICSIE DOMINVS PERPETVVS DE SAROS PATAK TOKAI REGECZ ECSED SOMLIO LEDNITZE SZERENCS ONOD.

The seal belonged to Ferenc Rákóczi II, leader of the fight for freedom (1703–1711) against the Habsburgs and 'Prince in command of the allied Estates of the Realm'; it dates, however, from the period which preceded this fight for freedom. As it is unequivocally stated in the inscription, the engraving was executed prior to 1700, since in 1701 the king caused Rákóczi to be arrested and imprisoned at Bécsújhely (Wiener Neustadt) for seeking an alliance with the French.

The maker of the seal was either the Swedish engraver, Daniel Warou, or the Nagy-bánya engraver, Daniel Ocsovay.

124 PIPE

Inv. No.: D.1974.153. Carved meerschaum
Length: 18 cm, height: 25 cm
1896

An ornamental pipe with silver-gilt mounts, decorated with the portraits of the twelve members of Dezső Bánffy's government. On the forepart of the bowl, surrounded by oval Neo-Gothic ornament, the busts of three men in Hungarian gala dress, supported by trumpeting angels with extended wings. Below these, in foliated scrolls are more men in gala dress, one in the centre and one on either side of him. Finally, in an open-work decoration of Gothic arabesque three more busts appear. The mounts of the pipe are set with precious stones in blue, red and green. A free-standing sculptured group on the cover of the bowl represents the raising of Prince Árpád on the shield. On the side of the stem of the pipe the name ADLER is stamped.

The pipe-case is of leather, bound and lined with blue velvet and blue satin; on the lining is the name and address of the makers: Fülöp Adler and Son, Budapest Deák Ferencz utcza 23, tooled in gold.

Pipes like these, fashionable in the last third of the nineteenth century, were designed as ornaments, not for use.

Date of foundation : 1802
Collections : Antique coins
Medieval and modern coins
Medals
Number of items : 238,961

DEPARTMENT OF COINS AND MEDALS

The basic material in the Department of Coins and Medals dates back to the earliest collections of the Museum; the 2,675 coins and medals, mainly Hungarian and Transylvanian, originally presented to the Museum by Ferenc Széchényi, form the nucleus of the collection as it stands today.

In the middle of the nineteenth century this material was enriched by further pieces from private collections, among them the coins and medals from the Jankovich, Weszerle and Ferenc Kiss collections which together constitute the basis for the Department's collection of coins from classical antiquity. The collection of southern Slavic coins from the Dobóczky collection received at the end of the last century, has raised the Department's various collections to an international standard.

The acquisition of the varied collection of the Hungarian painter, István Delhaes, marked a new phase in the history of the Department of Coins and Medals. Just under 20,000 pieces from this collection increased considerably the Department's stock of antique—mainly Greek—and Hungarian coins as well as its series of foreign medals. Private collectors of the twentieth century were more limited in their aims and confined themselves to attempts to achieve a complete collection of coins or medals based on a single theme. It was due to this attitude that the Department of Coins and Medals was able to add Miklós Dessewffy's barbarian coins and Béla Procopius's papal medals to its collection. The acquisition of these has meant that the Museum can now boast of possessing the most complete collection of Hungarian Celtic coins and papal medals in existence.

As a result of the Department's attitude to historical aspects of the subject in adding to its collections, new hoards are being preserved in their entirety. Although in the past hoards of outstanding importance had also been kept together—as in the case of the gold bars discovered at Krászna (Crasna), for instance—the determination to preserve entire hoards is, on the whole, a modern innovation. The hoard of Byzantine *solidi* at Szikáncspuszta and the contents of the Nagyharsány find which date from the eleventh century are both of quite extraordinary value to those engaged on historical research.

István Gedai

125 CELTIC TETRADRACHMA

Site: Egyházasdengeleg, Nógrád County
Inv. No.: L.I.1.1970.12. Silver, struck
Diameter: 21 mm, weight: 13.46 gm
2nd century BC

Obverse: bearded, laureate head of Zeus, turned right. Reverse: rider proceeding to the right; imitation lettering above the rider's head and in front of the horse.

The imitation Philippeus was made by a Celtic tribe who lived north-east of the Danube, more or less in what is today the territory of the Heves and Nógrád Counties. During their migrations they came into contact with the Greek coins of the Macedonian empire. Some of these they brought with them and used in the Carpathian Basin.

Owing to repeated copying as well as illiteracy, the inscription on the original Philippeus was gradually reduced and simplified into almost unrecognizable symbols.

These imitations cannot be dated with accuracy. Analysed stylistically they can be put into chronological order within a period beginning in 168 BC and ending with the Roman Conquest.

126 ERAVISCUS DENARIUS

Site: Budapest, Lágymányos, Pest County
Inv. No.: 70.1901.6. Silver, struck
Diameter: 17 mm, weight: 2.2 gm
c. 20 BC

Obverse: Head of Juno Sospita right, with trefoil behind the head. Reverse: the legend reads RAVIƧ, with a rudder and a globe.

The obverse is an imitation of that of the Papia gens (Babelon 2) denarius of the Roman Republic; the reverse is an imitation of the Cornelia gens (Babelon 54–55) denarius.

The Celtic Eraviscus tribe inhabited a large settlement at the foot of Gellért Hill in what is today Budapest, which is where a hoard of nearly 500 pieces of denarii was discovered. They include denarii of the Roman Republic itself, contemporary imitations of them and even imitations bearing the tribe's name: RAVIƧ (Eraviscus), the makers of the coins. The original republican denarii after which the near-contemporary copies were made, were minted between 80 and 70 BC. The Eraviscus denarii, which weigh somewhat lighter than the originals, can be dated round about 20 BC.

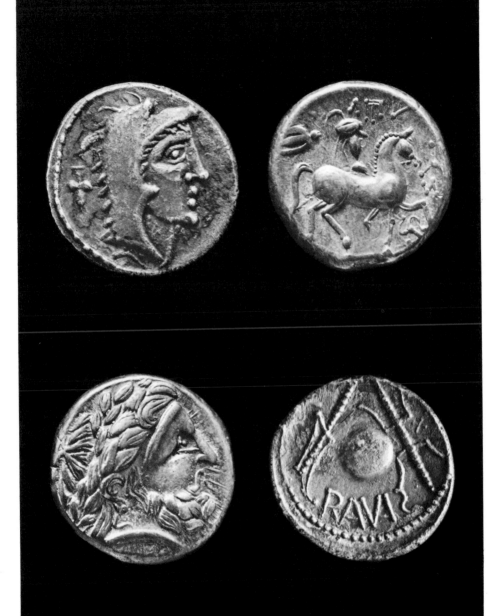

127 CLAY MOULD FOR CASTING COINS

Site: Komárom County
Inv. No.: 32.A/1901.3. Brick-coloured fired clay
Diameter: 47–55 mm
2nd century AD

Made in imitation of the obverse side of a Roman bronze coin. In the centre a bearded man's head turning to the left, surrounded by what purports to be a legend, in imitation lettering, incised.

From the second century quantities of forgeries of contemporary Roman coins were found in the Carpathian Basin. From the beginning of the third century colonial Greek bronze coins were common in the same area. It can be presumed that both the *limes* forgeries and the later colonial minted coins served as emergency currencies which could be used to substitute genuine bronze specimens which were becoming rare. The casting mould we see here belongs to this period. It was designed to imitate the bronze coinage of Antoninus Pius. Actual coins cast in this mould have not yet been found.

128 SILVER MEDAL OF THE EMPEROR VALENS

Site: Kiskőrös, Pest County
Inv. No.: 3/1971. Silver, struck
Diameter: 35–36 mm, weight: 12.78 gm
AD 367–375

This very rare medal came to the Department of Coins and Medals only a few years ago. Its interest lies in the fact that we know it was found in the Great Hungarian Plain.

The obverse displays the legend DN VALEN-S P F AVG bust draped, cuirassed, pearl diademed, right. On the reverse the legend TRIVMFATOR-GENT BARB; the Emperor, who is in military dress, advances to the right but turns his head to the left. In his left hand he holds a globe, in his right a *labarum*. Behind him kneels a captive, his head turned towards the Emperor. The medal was struck in Siscia. In ex. SISCPΣ, a multiplum (*cf.* RIC 8, for Valens and a variant of the mint-mark.)

The medal produced for Valens at the Siscia mint had not been known before; medals with the same obverse and reverse were struck at Treviri.

From Siscia the only medal known is a Valentinianus and that bears a mint-mark composed of a different combination. It is, however, probable that the Valens medal is a part of the same series and was also struck between AD 367 and 375.

129 ANTONINIANUS OF REGALIAN AND OF DRYANTILLA

Site: unknown
Inv. No.: Kiss 111; Bitnitz 788/a. Silver, struck
Weight: 3.85 gm and 2.17 gm, diameter: 19–20 mm and 10–11 mm respectively
Middle of the 3rd century

Regalian's Antoninianus came to the Department of Coins and Medals from the collection of Professor Ferenc Kiss in 1843. It is presumably a re-stamped specimen on which the obverse and reverse impressions are in the same positions as they were on the original coin. Thus it cannot be said which previous emperor's coin was re-stamped.

The obverse bears the legend IMP CPC [REGA]LIANVS AVG and the cloaked bust of an emperor with radiated head turned to the right. The reverse, inscribed ORIENS AVGG, shows Sol, full-face, raised right hand and a whip in the left (RIC 6). The Regalian coins are fairly rare. Most of the surviving specimens were found in Carnuntum and its surroundings.

The Dryantilla Antoninianus was acquired by the Museum through a legacy of Lajos Bitnitz, Provost of Szombathely, in 1872. It, too, is probably a re-stamped specimen, after, according to Göbl, the Julia Domna RIC 548 coin.

The obverse bears the legend SVLP DRYANTILL[A...] and the cloaked bust of the Empress in profile, turned right. The reverse is inscribed IVNON [...] and a figure holding a wreath and a sceptre (RIC 2).

130 STAMPED GOLD ROMAN BAR

Site: Kraszna (Crasna), Rumania
Inv. No.: 89/1888.1. Gold, cast
Length: 161 mm, width: 19–21 mm, thickness: 6–8 mm, weight: 338.8 gm
4th century

The bar was found near the village of Kraszna in 1887. The workmen who came upon what was manifestly an unprecedented find consisting of twelve such bars tried to sell the treasure through unofficial channels. In order to do this they broke four of the bars into fifteen pieces but eventually the authorities succeeded in gathering together some of the intact bars and some fragments. The whole bars and the nine broken pieces came to the Department of Medals.

The prism-shaped bar is stamped with rectangles framed by a beading. The *first stamp*, on the left, at the end of the bar, is horizontal and 22 × 11 mm in size. Its legend reads: LVCIANVS/OBR · I · SIC (and Christogram). The *second stamp*, also horizontal, is in the middle of the bar; it measures 23 × 11 mm. Here the beading encloses the busts of three cloaked emperors in full face wearing ornamental coronets. The heads on the right and in the middle are the same size, that on the left is much smaller. To the right of the three heads are the letters D D D, to the left, N N N, both groups stamped horizontally; the *third stamp* appears on the right hand end of the bar, set in a vertical position. It measures 22 × 11 mm and carries the stamped image of a female figure with an embattled crown, representing Sirmium. Seated, she is turned to the left and holds in her right hand a palm-branch—in her left a cornucopia. In the space in front of the figure, on a level with her head, is the Christogram; across the base, below her chair is the word SIRM. The bar was made in the Sirmium mint (now Mitrovica, Yugoslavia).

It is the second stamp with the heads of the three emperors which helps to determine the age of the gold bars. It was minted at the end of the fourth century.

131 SOLIDUS OF THEODOSIUS II

Site: Hódmezővásárhely, Szikáncspuszta, Csongrád County
Inv. No.: 28/1964.385. Gold. Weight: 4.50 gm, diameter: 20–21 mm
5th century

The find consisted of 1,439 solidus coins. Their total weight was nearly 6.5 kilograms, which corresponds to 20 Roman *libras*.

The find included two coins of Honorius and thirty-two of Valentinianus; the rest were solidi minted under Theodosius II. A few of the Valentinianus III solidi bear the mint-marks of Ravenna and Rome and one of the Theodosius II coins the mint-mark of Thessalonica, but the rest originated in the mint at Constantinople.

Obverse legend: DN THEODO-SIVS P F AVG; in the middle the half-length portrait of the bearded Emperor facing left. He wears a diadem and an imperial cloak and holds a map and a cross. The reverse bears the legend SECVRITAS-REIPVBLICAE and the seated figure of the Emperor seen from the front—a nimbus behind his head and a map and a cross in his hands. In the right field is a star; in ex. CONOB. The Szikáncs find can be dated on the evidence of the large number of coins with the legend IMP XXXXII COS-XVII P P it included and the representation of the city of Constantinople on the reverse. Theodosius II was seventeen times consul before the end of the year 443; his eighteenth consulship started in 444. Thus the coins discussed above must have been minted by 443 at the latest.

The closing date of the find coincides with the great Balkan military campaigns of Attila. It was at this time that the Byzantine court paid the Huns the arrears of the annual taxes which were owing. The treasures may, therefore, be regarded either a booty or as a part of the taxes which were paid.

132 KING STEPHEN'S DENARIUS

Site: Nagyharsány, Baranya County
Inv. No.: L.6/1975. Silver, struck. Diameter: 20 mm
Beginning of the 11th century

The coin was found at Nagyharsány in 1968. Altogether the find consisted of 80 coins, half of which belonged to this type. The legend on the obverse reads:+LANCEA REGIS. In the centre a hand holding a spear, on the reverse REGIA CIVITAS surrounding a Carolingian church, its frieze inscribed with the word REGI.

This denarius represents the start of Hungarian minting and as such is of decisive importance. The decoration at the Carolingian church on the reverse demonstrates the survival, among Hungarian goldsmiths, of a stock of patterns—which they continued to use in designing or making new objects. The palmette motifs seen earlier on sabretache plates, and designs taken from tenth-century jewellery reappear in the centre of the coin and on the outward-bending curves of the church gable. The legend on the reverse: REGIA CIVITAS is unequivocal evidence that the coin came from the King Stephen city mint; this can also be observed on his coins inscribed STEPHANVS REX.

133 GOLDGULDEN OF LOUIS THE GREAT

Site: Prijepolje, Yugoslavia
Inv. No.: 50/1939. Gold, struck. Diameter: 20 mm
c. 1370

In the thirties of this century a hoard, numerically small but significant, came to light at Prijepolje (east of Sarajevo) in Yugoslavia; it included two pieces of hitherto unknown goldgulden minted under Louis the Great of Hungary as well as a unique gold coin of István Tomasevič II, King of Bosnia (1461–1463).

The obverse of the gulden bears the legend LUDOVICI. D. G. UnGARIE and, in a lozenge, per fesse in the first, four bars (Hungary), the second *semis de fleurs de lis* (Anjou). The lozenge is enclosed in a Gothic rosette.

On the reverse is the standing figure of St. Ladislas, surrounded by the legend SAnTUS. LA-DISLAUS. R, and, on the side of the saint, the mint-mark P-G.

One of the two guldens minted with the same die, this is a precious example of the gold coins which became current in the twenties of the fourteenth century. It is valuable not only because of its numismatic rarity but also because of its stylistic interest and the ievidence it provides by the mark P-G (standing for Count Peter Chimle) which permits it to be dated with relative accuracy to about 1370; it can, at the same time, be considered to be a specimen of the last issue of the Buda goldguldens of Louis the Great.

134 GOLDGROAT COIN OF MATTHIAS I

Inv. No. 75/1933. Gold, struck
Diameter: 21.4 mm, weight: 6.99 gm
End of the 15th century

This unique coin came from the private collection of Duke Tassilo Festetich. It was retained by the Duke even after his collection had been put up for auction and it found its way, later, to the Museum as a donation by the Duke's son and heir.

The obverse bears the legend +MONETA MAThIE REGIS UNGARI and the Hungarian coat of arms. The arms, per cross quarterly, *sur-le-tout*, on an escutcheon, the Hunyadi raven.

The reverse is inscribed PATRONA–UNGARIE surrounding the Madonna and Child enthroned; on either side of her the mint-mark K-P.

The coin with a groat stamp in weight the equivalent of a double goldgulden plays a remarkable part in the history of Hungarian minting from several points of view. Matthias's monetary reforms, as a result of which permanent coins of good quality were minted, date from 1467. One characteristic was the arresting figure of the Madonna and Child on the face of both the denarii and the goldguldens as well as on that of the groats whose minting, which had been suspended by Louis the Great, was resumed. This unique gold coin was produced by means of the stamp of the popular groat.

135 HANS REINHART'S HOLY TRINITY MEDAL

Inv. No.: Ebenhöch 3909. Silver, cast
Weight: 276.5 gm, diameter: 102.5 mm
1544

This early specimen came to the Hungarian National Museum as a part of the collection of Canon Ebenhöch of Győr in 1889.

Obverse: in a plain border the legend PROPTER SCELUS POPULI MEI PERCUSSI EUM ESAIAE LIII. In the centre of the field is God the Father enthroned wearing the crown and mantle of the Holy Roman Empire and holding in his right hand a sceptre and in his left an orb. The field itself is powdered with the heads of cherubim. In front, reaching to a height above the knees of the Almighty, stands a cross bearing the Crucified Christ; on the horizontal beam of the cross is perched a dove—symbol of the Holy Spirit. Beneath the throne appear conventionalized cloud-symbols; on either side of the throne an angel kneels in adoration.

Reverse: the plain border bears the legend REGNANTE MAURITIO D G DUCE SAXONIAE JZC GROSSUM HUNC LIPSIAE HR CUDEBAT: AN^{no} MDXLIIII MENSE JANU. On either side of the central field an angel supports a shield in which there is an inscription of twenty-two lines. Below is a line of cloud-symbols.

The medal is the work of Hans Reinhart, the North German Renaissance master of epoch-making importance, His name was identified by Gersdorf in 1872 on the basis of the initials H R which appear on the medal. Hans Reinhart was born in 1510; in about 1539 he went to Leipzig and worked there for Johann Friedrich and later in the court of the Saxon Prince Moritz.

From the date included in the legend it can be seen that this famous Holy Trinity medal was completed in January 1544.

According to accounts published by specialists, seven original medals of this 1544 type are known.

136 100 DUCAT PIECE OF MIHÁLY APAFI, PRINCE OF TRANSYLVANIA

Inv. No.: Jankovich 246. Gold, struck
Diameter: 11.5 cm
1674

The Hungarian National Museum acquired this coin with the help of József, Elector Palatine of Hungary, in 1836, together with the Jankovich collection.

It is a gold plaque weighing a hundred ducats with stamped, in its centre, a ten-ducat piece surrounded by ten one-ducat pieces. The obverse of the ten-ducat piece bears the legend MICHAEL APAFI D G PRIN TRAN round a central waist-length portrait of the prince, in profile facing right. He wears a cap and a breastplate and holds a princely sceptre or mace in his right hand, a sword in his left. The reverse is inscribed PAR REG HVN DOM ET SIC CO 1674. In the centre is Apafi's coat of arms.

The obverse of the one-ducat piece is inscribed MI APAFI–D G PR T. In the centre is a portrait of the prince which somewhat resembles that on the ten-ducat stamp. The legend on the reverse reads: PAR REG HVN DO ET SIC 1674. Apafi's arms are stamped in the middle.

This rare one-hundred-ducat piece, known only by a few examples, was naturally not in circulation. Its true use can only be guessed at. The eastern part of Hungary— Transylvania—was separated from the main area of the country after the loss of the battle of Mohács (1526). The Transylvanian princes became dependants of Turkey and the high officials who carried some weight with the Sultan could be influenced only by gifts of gold disks stamped with the current coinage.

Those dating from the time of Apafi are especially associated with these historic events.

137 CROSS OF THE ROYAL HUNGARIAN ORDER OF ST. STEPHEN WORN BY MARIA THERESA

Inv. No.: 126/971.2. Gold and enamel with diamonds, rubies and emeralds
Diameter of the cross: 31.2 mm
1764

This royal Cross of the Order, set with precious stones, was originally deposited in the Vienna *Schatzkammer*, from which it found its way to the Hungarian National Museum with other objects of art which were transferred to Hungary in 1933.

The four points of the cross are composed of emeralds framed in gold. The round central field is bordered by a stripe of white enamel bearing the legend PUBLICUM MERITORUM PRAEMIUM. Within this, on a field of rubies, are set the initials M T (for Maria Theresa) in diamonds. Between the two letters, in emeralds, is the triple hill, symbol of Hungary, surmounted by a golden crown from which rises a patriarchal cross set with diamonds. The Order is suspended by an oval gold ring, also set with diamonds, and fastened to a violet ribbon striped with green.

The Order was founded by Maria Theresa on the occasion of the coronation of her son, later Joseph II, as King of Rome. It was awarded to those people of noble origin who "with their outstanding mental qualities and merits have distinguished themselves in the service of the Prince and the reigning dynasty". It was thus not a military but a civil decoration, designed as a reward for diplomatic services or artistic merit.

Only the cross made especially for the queen was set with precious stones. Those which were conferred as an award differed from it in that instead of being set with gems the cross was enamelled in white and bore on the reverse the legend STO ST RI AP (Sancto Stephani Regi Apostolico).

138 COLLAR AND ORDER OF THE GOLDEN FLEECE

Inv. No.: 53.33.1. Enamelled gold. Weight: 680 gm
19th century

The collar and pendant came into the possession of the Museum after World War II. The pendant—the Order's badge—is the fleece of a ram bound in the middle by a ring suspended from a sparking flint. The chain proper consists of alternating flints and steels, another device of the Order. In the example owned by the Museum these two devices are repeated thirty times.

The Order was founded in 1430 by Philip the Good, Duke of Burgundy, on the occasion of his wedding with his third wife, Isabella of Portugal. In a period when most of the royal houses of Europe had established their personal Orders of Chivalry, members of the Golden Fleece were, like members of other Orders, committed to defend their prince and to uphold the teaching of the Christian Church.

139 MILITARY CROSS OF DISTINCTION OF LAJOS KOSSUTH IN EXILE

Inv. No.: R.III.3155. Gold, enamelled. Weight: 14.30 gm, size: 39.8×39.2 mm
1849

Obverse: a gold Maltese cross enamelled in white. In the centre a green border surrounds the arms of Hungary. In the first, per fesse four bars; sinister a green hill crowned gold proper, above, the patriarchal cross. The green border bears the legend HŰ VITÉZSÉGÉRT A MAGYAR NEMZET (For faithful bravery, the Hungarian nation). Reverse: gold enamelled white with a green band in the centre inscribed SZABADSÁGHARCZ 1849 (War of Independence 1849).

This is a relic from the period of Kossuth's activities during his exile after the suppression of Hungary's fight for independence. In its form the cross corresponds to other decorations which existed at the same period but it did not represent a reward for outstanding military service during the actual time of the struggle.

The establishment of the decoration was ordered by the National Defence Committee in the autumn of 1848. According to a contemporary description it was to be worn as an enamelled gold cross suspended from a ribbon.

The rapid development of military events and the transfer of the government to Debrecen prevented the realization of a plan so costly in both materials and labour if Debrecen goldsmiths had been employed.

The fact that a few specimens were, nevertheless, produced much later appears from Kossuth's letter to Lajos Hentaller of 1891. During that year an exhibition of the relics of the fight for independence was being mounted in Budapest, and Hentaller, who was one of those responsible for the organization, wrote to Kossuth to ask him if he had any items which would be relevant. Kossuth sent his own cross which was not, however, identical with the one presented to the museum by János Pauer.

140 DANTE MEDAL

by Tamás Fekete
Inv. No.: 79/1973. Hammered silver
Weight: 138 gm, diameter: 101 mm
1968

This medal, hammered from a single sheet, showing the poet in profile facing left, was bought by the Museum's Department of Medals in 1973. Round the perimeter DANTE is inscribed on the left, ALIGHIERI on the lower right-hand side.

The medal was produced in 1968 while the artist was on a term of study in Florence.

One of the few surviving contemporary portraits of Dante represents the poet as a young man wearing a cap, his head turned left; another shows the poet as an old man, wearing a wreath of laurel. Tamás Fekete studied both contemporary representations but his medal is not a mechanical copy of any of the well-known portraits. He created, in fact, a new iconographical type by combining the two best-known portraits and shows the poet in profile in his old age, but wearing a cap. It is not of the poet laureate but of a man hardened in life's battles.

On this medal Dante looks out with tired lack-lustre eyes but his mouth and chin suggest energy, toughness and intransigence. Apart from its artistic merits the medal is both unique and remarkable in its method of production; instead of being cast or minted, the usual methods in this type of work, it was made by hammering the metal sheet.

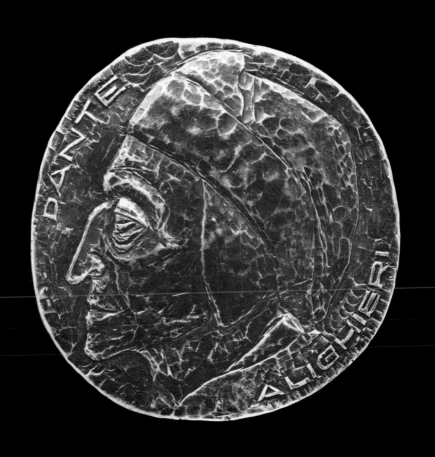

Date of foundation :	1884
Collections :	Paintings
	Drawings and engravings
	Photographs
Number of items :	57,500

HISTORICAL GALLERY

The Historical Gallery was founded through the initiative of the public and independently from the Museum. Its material was chosen from the collections of the National Museum and the Széchényi Library at the end of the eighties of the last century. It was only after long peregrinations that, at the end of World War II, the complete collection found its way back to its original home. It had, in previous decades, been housed in the Hungarian Academy of Sciences. The Gallery became a self-contained department of the National Museum in 1945.

The Historical Gallery's object is to collect and maintain pictorial source-material relevant to the history of Hungary. The paintings, drawings and prints are chosen primarily for their subjects and not on the basis of their artistic qualities. At the present time the Gallery relies more and more on photographs to provide historical records. The portraits in the collection represent the outstanding figures in the country's political and cultural life, while the views mainly show the development of Hungarian towns and cities. These two categories are reinforced by pictures representing important events in Hungary's history and pictures which record Hungarian national costume. The photographic collection is grouped in a similar way.

The collection of paintings, consisting of about 2,500 pictures, was rearranged in accordance with the modern system of storage in 1972; the new arrangement has greatly facilitated both the handling and the preservation of the material in good condition. Easy access to the very large and extremely important collection of prints, consisting of nearly 50,000 items, has been ensured by logical and systematic grouping of the material. Portraits and landscapes are filed in alphabetical order, according to subject, while pictures of historical events and of national costume are stored in chronological order. The collection has a graphic restoration workshop. Photographic material, which grew with exceeding rapidity after the Liberation of the country, was transferred to the Museum of the Labour Movement in 1964. Since 1971 the Hungarian National Museum has resumed the collecting of photographs.

The Historical Gallery is the most important centre of historical iconographic research.

György Rózsa

141 TWO VIEWS OF ESZTERGOM (Detail)

Etching by an unknown master after a drawing by Jakob Hoefnagel (1575–1630)
Size: 35.5 × 53.2 cm

The picture reproduced here appeared first in volume 5 of the *Civitates orbis terrarum* (Cities of the World) by G. Braun and F. Hogenberg, published in Cologne in 1597–1598. This book—a valuable source of cultural history—includes views of the most important cities of Europe with local figures in the foreground, in appropriate costume. The history of each town appears on the back of the illustration.

A foot-soldier appears in the upper part of the original picture, in the lower, gallant pikemen of the border castle. The fact that the artist has actually visited the scene depicted is confirmed by a description of it still to be found in the Bakócz Chapel. An English translation of the key to the specific places marked in the picture itself reads: A) Vineyards in Esztergom; B) Károly Hill; C) Rácváros; D) Fields of the Christian camps (at the recapturing of the city in 1595); E) Island; F) Hot baths; G) The tomb of a Turkish bey; H) Water Town; I) Turkish tombs; K) St. Thomas's Hill; M) Goggarn or Kakkatta (names of destroyed medieval villages which stood on the site of what is now Párkány); N) Esztergom Castle; O) Water Town; P) Rácváros; R) Island. The explanation of the letter L) in the upper picture is given on the reverse side as follows: "Costume of a loud-footed Hungarian soldier. Like other Hungarians, the soldiers wore hobnailed boots and, although they walked on tip-toe, the earth shook under their feet. They were brave and persevering in battle if the Turkish weapons compelled them to take vengeance but were better suited to fighting on horseback than as infantrymen."

STRIGONIVM. N. GRAN.

Hußaren

142 PORTRAIT OF THE LORD CHIEF JUSTICE, COUNT FERENC NÁDASDY

by Benjamin Block (1631–1690). Oil on canvas
Inv. No.: 2321
Size: 182×121 cm
1656

Ferenc Nádasdy, noted for his discriminating taste, was the richest and most broad-minded patron of the arts in the seventeenth century. Towards the end of his life he took part in the Wesselényi conspiracy and was beheaded in Vienna in 1671. He invited the Lübeck painter to Hungary from Vienna and commissioned from him the altarpieces in Győr and Loretto. The portrait of his wife, Anna Julianna Esterházy, also in the Gallery, is from the brush of the same painter. Block later went to Italy at Nádasdy's expense and subsequently held the position of court painter in Austria and Germany. Nádasdy's portrait is one of the finest seventeenth-century portraits of its kind in Hungary; apart from the features of his sitter, the painter was evidently interested in the costume he was wearing, which must have struck him as exotic. The picture is dominated by Nádasdy's gold-embroidered red pelisse.

Signed in the lower left-hand corner: "Beniamin Block ad viv. de pinxit A°. 1656".

143 RECAPTURE OF BUDA

by Romeyn de Hooghe (1645–1708). Etching
Size: 45.6 × 56 cm
1686

After 145 years in Turkish hands, Hungary's medieval capital was recaptured on September 2, 1686, following a siege of two months, by the international army under the command of Prince Charles of Lorraine. The event provoked wide repercussions throughout Europe and greatly affected public opinion everywhere; books and pamphlets discussing its significance were quick to appear. Descriptions of the siege and prints providing visual evidence based on such descriptions were soon published; from an artistic point of view Romeyn de Hooghe's is outstanding among them. This excellent Dutch master had never been to Hungary and, in delineating the scene, relied entirely on foreign models. Hooghe freely adapted, according to his own aesthetic taste, the composition he had borrowed from a view of the scene by an unknown German engraver. His print illustrated the smoking ruins of the castle of Buda as it must have appeared against its varied landscape background, itself enlivened by marching troops accompanying prisoners of war. In the foreground a group of Christian leaders directs the operations and receives the submission of representatives of the opposing Turks. This etching can be ranked among the finest examples of Dutch art relating to Hungary.

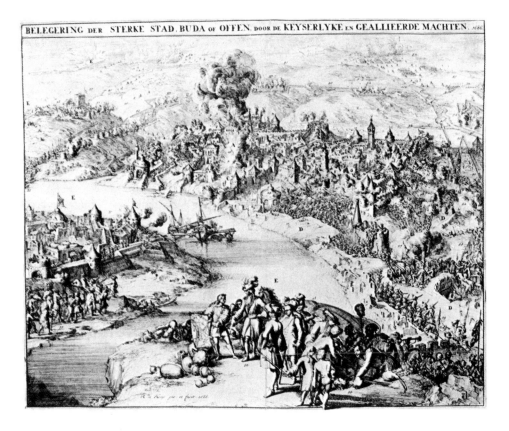

144 KURUC-LABANC BATTLE SCENE

Painter unknown
Inv. No.: T.6920. Gouache on paper
Size: 16×21.5 cm
First half of the 18th century

Kuruc soldiers in their typical uniform often appear in paintings and prints of the end of the seventeenth and the beginning of the eighteenth centuries. The popular Augsburg painter of battle scenes, Georg Philipp Rugendas, is the artist most frequently responsible for the copper engravings of this subject; oil paintings on the same theme also survive, most of them in Hungarian collections. On the evidence of their aesthetic quality some of them can be regarded as the work of Hungarian painters, but we cannot associate them with the names of any of the known artists.

The print reproduced here clearly reflects the tactics especially associated with *kuruc* warfare in which, in contrast to contemporary West European campaigns, individual bravery played an important role.

145 PORTRAIT OF FERENC LISZT

by Miklós Barabás (1810–1898). Oil on canvas
Inv. No.: 178
Size: 132×102 cm
1847

Miklós Barabás was one of the most popular Hungarian painters of the *biedermeier* period. He either painted or executed lithographic portraits of almost every one of his prominent contemporaries. His role in the development of the national art of Hungary is regarded as highly significant; a considerable proportion of his graphic works is included in the Historical Gallery's collection.

On his second visit to Pest Ferenc Liszt was received with all the honour due to a world-famous artist. The painting by Barabás, which was commissioned by the Historical Gallery Society for the Hungarian National Museum, was an added mark of respect. It successfully portrays the character of the great composer who was already celebrated all over Europe and is, at the same time, one of Miklós Barabás's masterpieces and a valuable item in Hungary's history of music.

Signed in the lower right-hand corner: "Barabás M. 847".

146 PORTRAIT OF LAJOS KOSSUTH

by August Prinzhofer (1817–1885). Lithograph
Size: 49.7 × 35.1 cm
1848

We owe this portrait of Kossuth, leader of the 1848–49 revolutionary fight for independence, to the lithographer August Prinzhofer, who had achieved prominence in Vienna. It is considered, from the artistic point of view, the best portrait of Lajos Kossuth. Prinzhofer was commissioned to undertake the work by a Budapest art dealer, József Wagner, who invited him to Pozsony (Bratislava) in January 1848 to execute portraits of the members of the National Assembly.

Apart from innumerable surviving copies, the popularity of the portrait is demonstrated by the fact that soon after its appearance it was rumoured that Kossuth had never sat to anyone else and that 50,000 copies of the print had been issued. We know today that these rumours were inaccurate.

147 THE BATTLE OF SZOLNOK ON THE 5TH MARCH, 1849

Lithograph by Charles de Fer after a drawing by Feodor August Dietz (1813–1870)

Size: 51 × 65.7 cm

The victory won by General Damjanich at Szolnok, the outstanding event in the spring campaign of the 1848–49 Hungarian War of Independence, was recorded in a series of lithographs entitled *Hungary in the Years 1848–1849*. In addition to the print reproduced here, two others have survived but the series was never completed. Its publisher, Miklós Szerelmey, worked as a lithographer in Pest in the 1840s; after the War of Independence he emigrated to London. For his series of lithographs of the war he enlisted the co-operation of several well-known artists who based their work on reports and sketches supplied by Hungarian eyewitnesses. Szerelmey also had contacts with Karl Marx and Friedrich Engels. The German text which was designed to publicize the lithographs was translated into English by Engels. It is a matter of great regret that Szerelmey's publication remained unfinished because it has deprived the iconography of the years 1848–1849 of reliable material of a high artistic standard.

148 THE BEGINNING OF THE CONSTRUCTION OF THE BUDAPEST METRO

by István Zádor (1882–1963). Ink on paper
Inv. No.: 73.241
Size: 360×260 mm
1950

The purchase of the drawings left by István Zádor, Kossuth prize-winner and a member of the Szolnok art colony, has enriched the collection of the Historical Gallery by the addition of new iconographical material on Hungary's recent past. These works of art reinforce the photographic evidence which has been growing in importance in recent years as a record of the period in which we live.

István Zádor's work includes drawings of every important political and cultural event which has taken place in Hungary between World War I and the 1950s. His drawings executed as a reporter during the 1918–19 revolution are of outstanding value.

The line drawing reproduced here shows the earthworks thrown up when the construction of the Budapest Metro line was begun.

Signed in the lower left-hand corner: "Zádor 1950 X 12".

Date of foundation: 1952
Subjects covered by the
collection: Archaeology
History
History of art
Preservation of monuments
Numismatics
Size of the collection: 87,345 items

CENTRAL ARCHAEOLOGICAL LIBRARY

The Central Archaeological Library was established as a department of the Hungarian National Museum in 1952 by the unification of the material preserved until then in different sections of the museum.

The scope of the library's activity covers the collection of literature relevant to the scientific research carried out in the museum. It also functions as a library of basic works on archaeology and numismatics at a national level.

In comparison to the initial stock of about 20,000 volumes, it must be noted that the present collection is approaching 90,000 works. In addition to purchases, this remarkable growth is due mainly to the development and extension of strong domestic and international relations between the library and corresponding organizations, and the exchange of the museum's publications with specialist literature published elsewhere. Today regular exchanges of material are maintained between the library and 616 Hungarian and foreign institutes.

Research in the fields covered by the library is greatly facilitated by its cataloguing system. The special documentary material consisting of the translation into Hungarian of articles published in foreign scientific reviews and the original manuscripts of Hungarian studies published only in a foreign language, is in itself a valuable collection.

The stock of microfilm primarily consisting of copies of foreign books indispensable to research but no longer available is similarly important.

Judit Sárdy

Date of foundation : 1951
Collections : Manuscripts
Records
Museum history
Photographs
Number of items : 213,200

DEPARTMENT OF RECORDS
AND DOCUMENTATION

Ever since the establishment of the Hungarian National Museum the Documentation Department has been the co-ordinating organ of archaeological research undertaken in this institution. The department's activities consist of collecting records of archaeology and work on excavation, the keeping of index-cards and the registration of private archaeological and numismatic collections. Since 1962 all excavations and their documentation, now obligatory, have been governed by ministerial decree. Documents in both these categories are also a part of the department's archives.

In addition to this work, the Documentation Department is responsible for the administration and co-ordination of all archaeological excavations in Hungary, as well as for the management of affairs connected with protected archaeological areas and private collections. The department also organizes preliminary surveys connected with new building projects. Apart from these duties it plays an important role in scientific research. Complete documentation of all archaeological excavations, including copies of material held by regional museums, is deposited in the department's archives, as well as documentation left by famous archaeologists of the past. Its section dealing with museum history collects and keeps records of every event connected with the building, history and exhibitions of the Hungarian National Museum since 1961.

The photographic archives include 50,000 negatives ranging from those of prehistoric material to medieval goldsmith's work. Up-to-date storage and methods of the handling of negatives have recently been introduced for the first time. Several thousands of photographs of irreplaceable art treasures, destroyed during World War II, are available in the archives of photographic prints to those working on research.

The Documentation Department is responsible for editing the *Régészeti Füzetek* (Archaeological Papers, series I and II), one of the Hungarian National Museum's publications.

Alice Sz. Burger

Date of foundation :   1953
Workshops :   General (ceramics, bone, glass, etc.)
                 Metal
                 Medals
                 Wood
                 Textile
                 Paper
                 Musical instruments

RESTORATION DEPARTMENT

In 1953 a Restoration Department was set up on the basis of the Museum's existing workshops and laboratories.

Conservation and restoration work has been undertaken in the Museum since the 1930s but for a long time after that date the restorers in the various fields were not armed with special qualifications.

After World War II restoration and conservation of seriously damaged works of art and other treasures became a matter of urgent necessity. In 1947 the Museum organized its first training course in conservation and restoration, which was attended by about 20 students.

Severely damaged material in the collections of the regional museums was also repaired gradually by teams of trained restorers. By the beginning of 1949 it was possible to mount an exhibition of objects which had been successfully restored to their former condition in the country's most important museum. Since 1969 conservation laboratories have been modernized and labour-saving equipment has been installed. Under the direction of qualified restorers the workshops and laboratories are now able to handle material of every kind.

Edit B. Thomas

149 RESTORATION OF THE SZEKSZÁRD VAS DIATRETUM

Site: Szekszárd, Tolna County
Inv. No.: 23.1847. Glass
Diameter of mouth: 15.9 cm, height: 11.6 cm
Roman Period, 4th century AD

This glass vessel from the Roman Period, found at Szekszárd in 1845, had to be taken apart and worked on from the beginning again because the added materials, used in the original restoration and now obsolete, had almost completely decayed and the original glass itself had suffered further deterioration.

In the first instance the vessel was taken to pieces and the old mixture of celluloid and chalk, used originally as a cement, was removed. Washing in fatty alcohol sulphonate revealed hair-cracks and layers of corrosion over the whole surface of the pieces of glass. After they had been neutralized and very slowly dried, the cleaned pieces showed an increase in transparency. The fragments were then laid out, matched, and the edges to be fitted together were stuck with an adhesive of synthetic resin with an *epoxi* base. After this process had been completed the small gaps which could still be seen on the two larger pieces required to be filled in. The mould was made of neutral dental wax and the small missing areas were filled in with *Eporezit R-3*.

To give a good surface-finish, the reconstructed glass walls were smoothed down and polished. The next stage in the restoration was the completion of the decorative motifs. Based on the design of the original two fish the missing third was reproduced using a silicon mould. The substitution of new letters for those missing from the legend was facilitated by the fact that every letter had survived in the parts which were intact. The letters and the network were cast from silicon moulds. Four letters, a fish and a part of the network on the *vas diatretum* are the only elements which have been reconstructed. A snail, two fish, five letters, the encircling network and most of the rim are composed of fragments glued together and filled in with the new synthetic resin.

150 THE RECONSTRUCTION OF THE DIADEM FROM CSORNA

Site: Csorna, Győr-Sopron County
Inv. No.: 55.36.1. Gold, set with cornelians and garnets
Length: 25.5 cm, width: 3.6 cm
Migration Period, 5th century

Originally the specimen was mounted on dark blue velvet onto which the fragments were stuck, side by side. To improve its scientific interest and bring it into line with modern methods of conservation these fragments were removed from the textile background by dissolving the organic adhesive with warm water. This was followed by appropriate cleaning, neutralization and drying.

In the first place the thin gold foil which formed the basis of the specimen was mounted onto a smaller bronze sheet by means of bending the gold over the edges of the bronze underplate. For the reconstruction a solution had to be found which, apart from ensuring the authenticity of the appearance of the gold diadem from an aesthetic point of view, would enable it to be well exhibited as completely stable. To achieve this, a drawing, prepared beforehand, was transferred to a hard brass sheet. After accurately marking the circumference, the original fragments were temporarily fixed onto this base. Where the gold foil was actually missing, the decoration was chased onto the brass plate. The motifs produced in this way produced, in reverse, a continuation of the embossed motifs which appeared on the gold foil, with the result that the reconstituted fragments were united into an aesthetic whole.

A flat support was riveted into the middle of the back of the brass under-plate. By using this devise the diadem can easily and safely be placed in an exhibition cabinet. The diadem was not bent into the exact form to fit the head but allowed to stand in a rather more open formation than would be usual in this type of jewellery, in order that, from the front, the maximum effect might be obtained.

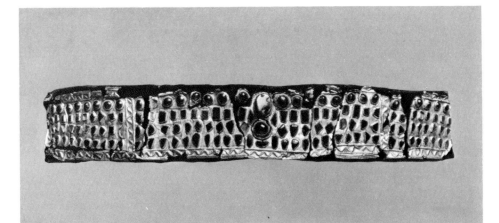

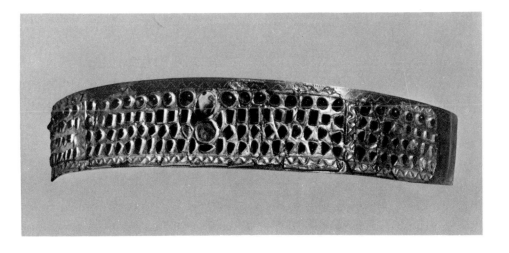

INSTITUTIONS AFFILIATED
TO THE HUNGARIAN NATIONAL MUSEUM

Date of foundation : 1965

THE VÉRTESSZŐLŐS OPEN AIR MUSEUM

The traces of the human settlement discovered at Vértesszőlős by specialists examining the limestone in the local quarry in 1962 were excavated in the years between 1963 and 1968 by László Vértes. In the area they found various traces of human settlement and excavated two archaeological and one palaeontological sites in their entirety. The once extant travertine basins formed by the one-time tepid-water springs, which dried out periodically, made a good home for man, and as a result of lengthy activity, a rich settlement came into being. The early men used flint and quartz river-pebbles to make their 3–4 cm long tools. After consuming the meat of their prey—large herbivorous, they cut the bones to get at the marrow and used the fresh, fatty bones to feed their fires. A close study of the several thousands of tools excavated from either stratified accumulations or cemented layers gives a good picture of the development of man's intellect and manual dexterity.

Viola T. Dobosi

151 VÉRTESSZŐLŐS
Site 1, where the cranial bone of the Archanthropus was found

In the *Mindel interstadial sediment* an accumulation of compact layers of the bones of slaughtered herbivorous animals was found; at the same time both pebble-tools and traces of human remains were discovered: the fragments of a tooth of a seven-year old child, Homo I, and an occipital bone of an adult, Homo II. The latter were identified by Andor Thoma as *Homo (erectus seu sapiens) palaeohungaricus n.ssp.* The occipital bone is triangular in shape. Its main characteristic is the occipital ridge which runs along its outer surface. The traces of a fracture visible near the *foramen magnum* indicate that the base of the skull had been removed for a cult purpose, designed to capture the spirit or the physical strength of the deceased. The find belongs to the Archanthropus group, analogies of which are the Mauer jaw in Europe, the Tsoukoutien finds, the Trinil calvaria in Asia, and the human remains in Olduwai, Africa. Its age can be placed at 300,000 to 400,000 years.

The footprints, unmatched elsewhere, found at Site III are of similar age. They belong to the animals (bison, bear, rhinoceros and deer) that came to drink at the spring there. These traces were preserved by the rapid precipitation of lime. The rare geological structure of the basin, the fireplaces, the footprints and the rich strata consisting of five separate cultural levels are phenomena which cannot be found in a similar combination elsewhere in the world.

The Hungarian National Museum developed the site into an *in situ* exhibition, where, beneath protective buildings, one of the most ancient settlements in Europe can be studied in its original position.

Date of foundation:	1950
Collections:	Archaeology
	History
	Archives
Number of items:	51,686

KING MATTHIAS MUSEUM, VISEGRÁD

Visegrád Museum is the collective name covering a group of monuments composed of three large units. The first is the castle's fortification system and includes the donjon; the second is the Citadel, and the third, the ruins of the Royal Palace. The new museum building, which is now under construction, is designed to integrate the three units, each of which has a long tradition behind it. The tower has been identified as the one-time prison of King Salamon, the citadel as the repository for the coronation regalia while the palace was the scene of the attempt on the life of the King by Felicián Zách in 1330 and, following it, of the most sanguinary reprisal of the period. The interest of the visitor will inevitably be aroused, in the first instance, by the ruins; work on salvaging and restoring them had already started over a hundred years ago, when Imre Henszlmann and Frigyes Schulek carried out valuable work on them. János Schulek and Kálmán Lux distinguished themselves in the same connection between 1927 and 1945. Among these restorers János Schulek has won a lasting place in history for the dedication and perseverance with which he fought against complete lack of understanding on the part of authorities, until on December 31, 1934 his unshakable conviction in the face of innumerable difficulties was at last rewarded by the discovery of the first building in the palace complex—the court of honour.

Originally it was intended that the donjon should be restored as a royal hunting lodge. Its restoration as a museum was first proposed by the Castle Committee sometime in the 1930s or 40s. When, after the Liberation of Hungary, the complex of monuments came into the ownership of the State, its reconstruction as a museum was begun in 1950.

Large-scale excavations, carried out under the direction and with the material support of the National Board of Historic Monuments, revealed the layout of the whole complex from a topographical point of view as well as the history of the construction of the lower castle and of the Citadel. Year by year, more and more of the complex of monuments was unearthed while, at the same time, new publications, based on factual evidence deduced from the excavations, superseded the rather more romantic literature of an earlier date.

Miklós Héjj

Visegrád assumed an important role in the reign of Charles Robert of Anjou (1308–1342) when the royal court moved there in 1316 and the King began the building of the palace on a site between the lower fortress and the town. It was finished by 1335, the year of the Visegrád Congress at which the Hungarian, Polish and Bohemian kings and the leaders of the Teutonic Order were participants. The second phase of the palace's development is associated with Louis the Great (1342–1382) and is recognizable by the Franco–Italian style which was by that time widespread. The ground-plan as it is known soday dates from this period. It consists of three related units: on the northern side ttood the many-storeyed palace of the King, south of it, the large palace of the Queen, the two joined by a chapel thirty-five metres in length. At the turn of the fourteenth century King Sigismund extended the palace in the direction of the Danube and, from a document surviving from 1474, it is clear that construction was resumed under King Matthias Corvinus; Galeotto Marzio, writing between 1484 and 1486, refers to it as already completed. From the point of view of both art and architecture, the palace reached its apotheosis in rich decoration during this period. The late Gothic cloister in the court on the level of the second terrace, the red marble fountain, the lower outer court and the system of monumental attached stairways date from this time. The carved decoration of the red marble fountain of Hercules in the court of honour bears witness to the high level of Hungarian taste in the field of Renaissance sculpture. The decorative elements of the fountain represent the struggle between the infant Hercules and the hydra of Lerna. It is probably the work of Tomaso Fiamberti.

Miklós Oláh, the humanist, has left us a colourful description of the splendour of the palace of King Matthias at Visegrád, praising, among other things, the fountains which decorated its courts. So far five have been excavated. The finest was found in 1955 on the fourth terrace of the palace. An exact replica of it now stands on the place formerly occupied by the original.

It is a wall-fountain, supported by five crouching lions, each attacked by a small dog. A column resting on the back of each lion, cylindrical below and hexagonal above, supports the quatrefoil basin of the fountain which is attached to the wall at the back. A tall embattled baldachin, supported on Gothic arcading, rises from the hexagonal capitals of the columns; five of the eight arches rest on these, the other arches terminate in finials each decorated with a lion's head. Within the baldachin the Hunyadis' coat of arms decorates its ceiling. The winged crest is surrounded by an incomplete legend which seems to indicate that the fountain was built in 14.3—probably standing for 1473. In the broad frieze, above the arches on the outside, appear eight shields with the arms of Hungary, Dalmatia, Silesia, Bohemia, Moezia, Moravia, Luxembourg and Lausitz. The wall at the back of the fountain bears the coats of arms of the King's kinsmen— the Szilágyis, the Zápolyas and the Bellyényis. The water, or according to chroniclers, on the occasions of royal receptions, the red and white wine, flowed into the red marble basin from two spouts in the form of lions' heads placed at mid-height on the wall.

This red marble fountain was produced in the royal workshop at Visegrád.

Date of foundation: 1950
Collections: Archaeology
Numismatics
Ethnography
Art
Applied art
History
Archives
Number of items: 16,558

THE RÁKÓCZI MUSEUM, SÁROSPATAK

Sárospatak Castle is among Hungary's most precious monuments, inseparable from the nation's history and those progressive features in its former struggles for independence.

The earliest parts of the Castle were built at the end of the fifteenth century by the Pálóczi family. Between 1534 and 1542 it was added to by Péter Perényi, by which time the complex consisted of an outer fortification system, an inner fortress and the castle proper. The architecture of the castle, with which several names are associated, displays a rich assortment of late Renaissance sculptural decoration executed in the sixteenth century. Péter Perényi renovated the keep or Red Tower and the eastern wing of the castle, adding splendid ornamental framing to windows, doors and fireplaces. The most spectacular part of the castle is the Lorántffy loggia, a monument we owe to György Rákóczi I and Zsuzsanna Lorántffy, who from 1641 further developed the castle in a manner which befitted their princely status. The Red Tower was connected by a closed corridor supported on arches with the east wing of the castle. The finest part of the loggia is the decorative Renaissance window frame which bears the date 1506; as an additional ornamental feature it was subsequently attached to this part of the original building.

The castle was the scene of many an event of national importance. The peace of Nagyvárad was drawn up here by the envoys of Emperor Ferdinand and János Zápolyai in 1537. Here István Bocskai received the envoys of the Sultan bringing him the crown. The greatest days of the castle are connected with Ferenc Rákóczi II. It was in this castle that the fight for freedom against the Habsburgs came to fruition. Here the Prince held his last Diet in 1708. As a result of the land reforms of 1945 Sárospatak Castle came into state ownership and in 1950 a museum was set up on the premises. Its more than forty rooms are visited by an average of over 200,000 visitors a year. Among the collections housed here the historic objects associated with the Rákóczis, the tangible remains from serfdom on the Rákóczi estates, as well as the glass, porcelain and pottery workshops, are of outstanding interest.

Ákos Janó

This charming piece of architecture is the loveliest among the remains of the Lorántffy wing of Sárospatak Castle. The stellar vault forms a light umbrella-roof over a small round room in the north-east corner of the castle. The ribs of the vaulting are in the form of thorny rose-branches which converge on the stucco rosette enclosed in a rectangular frame in the middle of the ceiling. Six spear-like formalized leaves project at either side of the central rosette. The vault itself is painted with grotesques which include stylized flowers and foliage on a white ground, designed in a style reminiscent of contemporary embroidery. Human heads emerge from the cups of flowers and dancing figures appear among vases of flowers, birds and four-footed animals. Although allegorical figures certainly occupy the lunettes between the arches of the vaulting, only the figure representing Power is identified by an inscription—"Potestas". Fame is represented by a winged youth riding on a globe as he blows a trumpet, and Plenty by a female figure holding a cornucopia. Below them is a border in which appear painted scenes of hunting, also reminiscent of embroidery. In the lunette over the central window are three coats of arms, supported by two youths: on the left, the arms of Hungary, on the right of Bohemia and in the centre the arms of the Lorántffy family. From these it can be inferred that the bay window was painted for the occasion of the wedding of Prince Zsigmond, youngest son of György Rákóczi I and Zsuzsanna Lorántffy, which took place at Sárospatak in 1651.

The bay window has associations with the Wesselényi conspiracy against the Habsburg rule, planned in 1670 in an effort to recover Hungary's independence.

With Péter Perényi's grandiose architectural schemes, Sárospatak Castle became Hungary's most dignified Late Renaissance building. The chief aim of its owners was to render the castle, whose fortifications were modern for their period, a seat worthy of the Rákóczi family. It was in the spirit of these aspirations that the *bokály* house was conceived and built. In the course of the excavations of 1965 small fragments of its original tiles were found.

The Hungarian term *bokály* designates the glazed wall-tiles used in the East, known in Turkish as *cini*. Walls of palaces and mosques in the Muslim world had been covered with these tiles since the thirteenth century. At the end of 1641 the Transylvanian Prince, György Rákóczi I, ordered the hall on the third floor of the Red Tower, which was to be rebuilt after a gunpowder explosion, to be covered with tiles of this kind. They were produced in the workshops of the same masters who had produced the tiles for the Sultan's Bagdad Kiosk in his palace in Constantinople, and were brought to Sárospatak by Rákóczi's emissaries. From the surviving fragments of the tiles, which are decorated with pomegranates and scrolls of flowers, four pieces form a complete unit in the repeat pattern. Their various shades of blue create a three-dimensional effect. To cover the hall, 9 metres long and 4.5 metres wide, to a height of 2.75 metres, 800 whole tiles and 160 skirting tiles were used.

This splendid tiling was, however, short-lived. After the Wesselényi conspiracy the imperial army wrecked the castle and in 1702 the blowing up of its outer fortifications completely destroyed the *bokály*-decorated house.

Date of foundation :   1949

THE KOSSUTH MEMORIAL MUSEUM, MONOK

Lajos Kossuth was born in this house on September 19, 1802. The museum it now enshrines keeps his memory fresh.

The manor house in Neo-Classic style was built at the very beginning of the nineteenth century.

However, Lajos Kossuth's parents left this gently sloping forest-clad hilly region as early as 1803.

Kossuth became the spiritual leader of the Hungarian people during the era of reform—a steadfast revolutionary who, by the spoken word as in his writings, fought for the liberation of the serfs and for equal rights for all men. He was the greatest Hungarian orator, leader of the revolution and fighter in the struggle for freedom which broke out on March 15, 1848; he had long realized that if Hungary were to gain her independence the Habsburgs must be overthrown. As governor he occupied the highest constitutional position for the second time during a transitional period in Hungary's history.

After the failure of the War of Independence, defeated by the combined European reactionary forces, Kossuth lived the bitter life of an exile. As changes in the political situation took place, his hopes gradually diminished but until his death in Turin in 1894 he never ceased to believe staunchly in the cause of Hungary's independence.

The memorial museum exhibits the most important phases of Kossuth's career in the form of both written documents and various objects related to him.

József Korek

LIST OF PLATES

(The italicized names indicate authors of the description of the Plates)

1 Laurel-leaf shaped point (Szeleta Cave). *Viola T. Dobosi*
2 Shell bracelets (Kisköre). *István Ecsedy*
3 Bowl with pedestal (Lebő, Alsóhalom). *István Ecsedy*
4 Wagon-shaped vessel (Szigetszentmárton). *István Ecsedy*
5 Human-shaped urns (Ózd, Center). *István Ecsedy*
6 Bell-shaped beaker (Tököl). *Tibor Kovács*
7 Bracelet (Dunavecse). *Tibor Kovács*
8 Bronze hatchet (Mezőkomárom). *Tibor Kovács*
9 Bronze bucket (Hajdúböszörmény). *Tibor Kemenczei*
10 Urn (Nagyberki). *Tibor Kemenczei*
11 Stag-shaped shield ornament (Mezőkeresztes, Zöldhalompuszta). *Tibor Kemenczei*
12 Bronze rattles (Nagytarcsa). *Tibor Kemenczei*
13 Vessel with handles decorated with heads of bulls (Kósd). *Tibor Kovács*
14 Gold beads decorated with masks (Szárazd-Regöly). *Tibor Kovács*
15 Bronze statue of Victory (Akasztó). *Endre Tóth*
16 Bronze lamp decorated with a bust of Jupiter (Mór). *Éva Bónis*
17 Veriuca's tombstone (Dunaújváros). *Sándor Soproni*
18 Pair of silver brooches (Pátka). *Éva Bónis*
19 *Terra sigillata* vase (Tác). *Éva Bónis*
20 Model of a gateway (Dunapentele). *Éva Bónis*
21 Jupiter Dolichenus plaque (Dunakömlőd). *Sándor Soproni*
22 *Fondo d'oro* (Dunaújváros). *Endre Tóth*
23 Bronze casket mounts (Kisárpás). *Éva Bónis*
24 Bust of Valentinian II (Pécs). *Sándor Soproni*
25 Ornamental brooch (Szilágysomlyó, Şimleul-Silvaniei). *Ilona Kovrig*
26 Ceremonial cauldron (Törtel). *Ilona Kovrig*
27 Coronet (Csorna). *Ilona Kovrig*
28 Cicada-shaped brooches (Györköny). *Ilona Kovrig*
29 Bracelets (Dunapataj, Bakodpuszta). *Ilona Kovrig*
30 Brooches (Szentendre). *Ágnes Sós*
31 Disk-shaped brooch (Keszthely, Fenékpuszta). *Ágnes Sós*
32 Crescent-shaped earring. *Attila Kiss*

69 Earthenware jug (Szécsény). *Nándor Parádi*
70 Guild badge (Brassó [Braşov]). *Judit Kolba*
71 Renaissance jewellery. *Judit Kolba*
72 Goblet with cover. *Judit Kolba*
73 Turkish silver cup. *Géza Fehér*
74 The Brózer chalice (Kolozsvár [Cluj-Napoca]). *Judit Kolba*
75 The Rákóczi tankard. *Judit Kolba*
76 Bálint Frank's tankard and cover (Nagyszeben [Sibiu]). *Judit Kolba*
77 Throne-carpet. *Mária Ember*
78 Chasuble (Sztropkó). *Mária Ember*
79 Lady's gown and chemise. *Mária Ember*
80 Man's gown and chemise. *Mária Ember*
81 Chasuble (Kőszeg). *Katalin F. Dózsa*
82 Chasuble. *Mária Ember*
83 Lady's gala dress. *Mária Ember*
84 Table-cloth. *Mária Ember*
85 Lady's dress. *Mária Ember*
86 Lady's gala dress. *Mária Ember*
87 Child's suit and high cap. *Mária Ember*
88 Gentleman's gala suit. *Mária Ember*
89 Lady's evening dress. *Katalin F. Dózsa*
90 Lady's evening gown. *Katalin F. Dózsa*
91 Backgammon board. *Annamária T. Németh*
92 Covered tankard. *Annamária T. Németh*
93 Covered goblet. *Annamária T. Németh*
94 Jewellery to be worn with full dress. *Annamária T. Németh*
95 'Ivory' saddles. *Ferenc Temesváry*
96 Ornamental papal sword of King Wladislas II. *Ferenc Temesváry*
97 Suit of armour of Louis II, King of Hungary. *Ferenc Temesváry*
98 Sámuel Teleki's saddle. *Ferenc Temesváry*
99 Broadsword and sabre of János Kemény, Prince of Transylvania. *Ferenc Temesváry*
100 Powder-horns. *Ferenc Temesváry*
101 Gun and attachments, in a case. *Ferenc Temesváry*
102 Cupboard. *Imre Bánkúti*
103 Writing cabinet. *Imre Bánkúti*
104 Armchair. *Imre Bánkúti*
105 Guild chest. *Imre Bánkúti*

106 Jug. *Edit Haider*
107 Dish. *Edit Haider*
108 Spice jar. *Edit Haider*
109 Round dish. *Edit Haider*
110 Jug. *Edit Haider*
111 Flasks. *Edit Haider*
112 Flower bowl with perforated cover. *Edit Haider*
113 Fish-server. *Edit Haider*
114 Virginal. *György Gábry*
115 Cembalo. *Eszter F. Gát*
116 Barytone. *György Gábry*
117 Harp. *György Gábry*
118 Pianoforte. *György Gábry*
119 Pocket watch. *Eszter F. Gát*
120 Seal (Esztergom). *Ferenc Szakály*
121 Seal. *Ferenc Szakály*
122 Gold seal. *Ferenc Szakály*
123 Seal. *Ferenc Szakály*
124 Pipe. *Edit Haider*
125 Celtic tetradrachma (Egyházasdengeleg). *Katalin B. Sey*
126 Eraviscus denarius (Budapest). *Katalin B. Sey*
127 Clay mould for casting coins (Komárom). *Katalin B. Sey*
128 Silver medal of the Emperor Valens (Kiskőrös). *Katalin B. Sey*
129 Antoninianus of Regalian and of Dryantilla. *Katalin B. Sey*
130 Stamped gold Roman bar (Krászna [Crasna]). *Katalin B. Sey*
131 Solidus of Theodosius II (Hódmezővásárhely, Szikáncspuszta). *Katalin B. Sey*
132 King Stephen's denarius (Nagyharsány). *István Gedai*
133 Goldgulden of Louis the Great (Prijepolje). *István Gedai*
134 Goldgroat coin of Matthias I. *István Gedai*
135 Hans Reinhart's Holy Trinity medal. *Vera G. Héri*
136 100 ducat piece of Mihály Apafi, Prince of Transylvania. *István Gedai*
137 Cross of the Royal Hungarian Order of St. Stephen. *Vera G. Héri*
138 Collar and Order of the Golden Fleece. *Vera G. Héri*
139 Military cross of distinction of Lajos Kossuth in exile. *Vera G. Héri*
140 Dante medal. *Vera G. Héri*
141 Two views of Esztergom. *György Rózsa*
142 Portrait of Count Ferenc Nádasdy. *György Rózsa*

MEMBERS OF THE RESEARCH STAFF
(on the 1st January 1977)

DIRECTORSHIP

Ferenc Fülep	*D.Sc. Director-General*
József Korek	*Deputy Director-General, candidate in historical studies*
István Tamás	*Ph.D. Deputy Director-General, historian*
István Fodor	*Research Secretary, archaeologist*
Jolán Dolniczky	*Financial Director*

DEPARTMENT OF ARCHAEOLOGY

Ilona Kovrig	*Head of Department, candidate in historical studies*
Éva B. Bónis	*Ph.D. Deputy Head of Department, candidate in historical studies*
Viola T. Dobosi	*Ph.D. Archaeologist*
Éva S. Garam	*Ph.D. Archaeologist*
Tibor Kemenczei	*Ph.D. Archaeologist, candidate in historical studies*
Attila Kiss	*Ph.D. Archaeologist*
Ágnes Cs. Sós	*Ph.D. Archaeologist, candidate in historical studies*
Ilona Stanczik	*Archaeologist*
Endre Tóth	*Ph.D. Archaeologist*
István Vörös	*Historical Zoologist*
Zsuzsa K. Zoffmann	*Anthropologist*

MEDIEVAL HISTORY DEPARTMENT

Emese S. Nagy	*Head of Department, Archaeologist*
Zsuzsa S. Lovag	*Ph.D. Deputy Head of Department, art historian*
István Dienes	*Ph.D. Archaeologist*
Géza Fehér	*Ph.D. Art Historian*
Ibolya Gerelyes	*Archaeologist*
Judit H. Kolba	*Ph.D. Art Historian*
Julia Kovalovszki	*Ph.D. Archaeologist*
Károly Mesterházy	*Ph.D. Archaeologist, candidate in historical studies*
Nándor Parádi	*Ph.D. Archaeologist*
András Pálóczy-Horváth	*Ph.D. Archaeologist*

MODERN HISTORY DEPARTMENT

Imre Bánkúti	*Ph.D. Head of Department, candidate in historical studies*
István Berta	*Deputy Head of Department, Historian*
Katalin F. Dózsa	*Ph.D. Art Historian*
Eszter F. Gát	*Historian of Musical Instruments*
Edit Haider	*Ethnographer*
Annamária T. Németh	*Art Historian*
Ferenc Szakály	*Ph.D. Historian, candidate in historical studies*
Ferenc Temesváry	*Ph.D. Historian*
Károly Vigh	*Ph.D. Historian*

DEPARTMENT OF COINS AND MEDALS

István Gedai	*Ph. D. Head of Department, candidate in historical studies*
Vera G. Héri	*Ph. D. Numismatist*
Katalin B. Sey	*Ph. D. Numismatist*

HISTORICAL GALLERY

György Rózsa	*Ph.D. Head of Department, candidate in art historical studies*
Gizella C. Wilhelmb	*Ph.D. Art Historian*

CENTRAL ARCHAEOLOGICAL LIBRARY

Sándor Soproni	*Ph. D. Head of Department, candidate in historical studies*
Judit Sárdy	*Deputy Head of Department, Chief Librarian*
Mária F. Fejér	*Librarian*
Éva Moskovszky	*Ph. D. Chief Librarian*

DEPARTMENT OF RECORDS AND DOCUMENTATION

Alice Sz. Burger	*Ph. D. Head of Department, Archaeologist*
Pál Patay	*Ph. D. Deputy Head of Department, Archaeologist*
Éva V. Kocztur	*Ph. D. Archaeologist*
Éva Hoppál	*Librarian*

RESTORATION DEPARTMENT

Edit B. Thomas	Ph. D. Head of Department, Archaeologist
Géza Báthy	Deputy Head of Department, Chief Restorer
Sándor Baski	Restorer
Katalin T. Bruder	Chief Restorer
László Hegedűs	Restorer
Erzsébet Hidvégi	Restorer
Judit N. Lőrincz	Restorer
Irén A. Sós	Restorer
László Szabó	Restorer
László Szarvas	Restorer

PUBLIC EDUCATION SECTION

Márta T. Lovas	Head of Section, Historian
Szilvia Bedő	Historian
László Borsányi	Ethnographer

KING MATTHIAS MUSEUM, VISEGRÁD

Miklós Héjj	Ph. D. Director, Archaeologist
Dániel Grooh	Archaeologist
Mátyás Szőke	Archaeologist
Imre Tavas	Chief Restorer

THE RÁKÓCZI MUSEUM, SÁROSPATAK

Ákos Janó	Ph. D. Director, Ethnographer
Katalin J.	Dankó Archaeologist

THE KOSSUTH MEMORIAL MUSEUM, MONOK

Tibor Zsuffa	Director

CONTENTS